GRAMMATICAL FORM AND GRAMMATICAL MEANING
A tagmemic view of Fillmore's deep structure

NORTH-HOLLAND
LINGUISTIC SERIES   5
Edited by S. C. DIK and J. G. KOOIJ

GRAMMATICAL FORM AND GRAMMATICAL MEANING

A tagmemic view of Fillmore's Deep Structure Case concepts

JOHN T. PLATT

Department of Linguistics
Monash University

1971

NORTH-HOLLAND PUBLISHING COMPANY
AMSTERDAM · LONDON

Library of Congress Catalog Number 72-166313

ISBN 0 7204 6185 5

Publishers:

NORTH-HOLLAND PUBLISHING COMPANY – AMSTERDAM
NORTH-HOLLAND PUBLISHING COMPANY, LTD. – LONDON

PRINTED IN THE NETHERLANDS

PREFACE

A preface is always difficult to write. It often fails to mention and thank those who ought to be mentioned and thanked and the problem of order is just as difficult. Therefore I shall mention but a few names and those in a roughly chronological order.

Firstly I am indebted to Professor Ruth Brend, University of Michigan, for valuable discussion on tagmemic theory and for introduction to works by A.L. Becker and C.J. Fillmore.

To various members of staff, both academic and non-academic, of various departments at Monash University I extend my thanks for their patience in answering my questions on acceptability. I am indebted to Professor G. Hammarström, Monash University, for his detailed criticism of the earlier version before it was presented as a doctoral thesis at Monash University.

Professor K. Pike read the work in its thesis form and Professor R. Long-acre also made valuable suggestions, some of which have been incorporated in this revised version. Other modifications have been made as the result of criticism and suggestions from Professor Simon C. Dik and Dr. J.G. Kooij, University of Amsterdam, to whom I express my sincerest thanks.

Lastly, I could not fail to mention the help of my wife, Dr. Heidi K. Platt, Monash University. To her I am indebted for German exemplification, critical examination of the work and invaluable help in preparation for publication.

John T. Platt

Monash, December 1970

CONTENTS

1. INTRODUCTION

1.0. Choice of method

This work is based on the claim that besides the 'overt' syntactic relationships in any particular language there are also meaning relationships. In recent years there have been a number of investigations, particularly using a generative transformational approach, that have recognized a deep structure underlying surface structure phenomena in syntax.

Although Pike recognized early in his work the importance of semantics in syntactic analysis, formal semantic considerations were only given to the tagmemic method at a recent stage in its development (see Becker 1967). For the present investigation into Grammatical Meaning I have chosen the tagmemic model. The choice was made for two reasons. Firstly, the nature of the tagmeme as a unit, particularly as suggested by Pike and developed by Becker, lends itself with its combination of function and filler to the further development of a semantic component for both parts of the unit. Secondly, the tagmemic approach to syntax, working with the concept of various levels, makes it possible to single out a particular level for consideration at any one time.

1.1. Standard concept of the tagmeme. Functions

The standard concept of the tagmeme is that of a unit composed of function and filler. Functions of tagmemes vary according to the syntactic level of analysis. For instance, the clause construction

The fat boy consumed all the biscuits

consists of three tagmemes: (1) Subject tagmeme: filled by a noun phrase; (2) Predicate tagmeme: filled by a transitive verb; (3) Object tagmeme: filled by a noun phrase.

1

Clauses that have the same number and type of tagmemes would belong to a certain clause type. For example the Active Transitive clause type in English may be stated as follows:

$$+ S : \text{n.phr.} \quad + P : \text{vtr.} \quad + O : \text{n.phr.}^{[1]}$$

The + sign indicates that the tagmemes are obligatory to this particular clause type. Tagmemes which may optionally appear are marked ±, for instance:

$$\pm M \quad (\text{referring to a modifier, e.g. 'this evening').}$$

Given a clause type formula of the following nature: [2]

$$+ S \quad + P \quad \pm M_1 \quad \pm M_2 ,$$

three operations can be carried out in the following order:
(1) reading or R-operations;
(2) permutation or P-operations;
(3) exponence or E-operations.

1.1.1. *R-operations*
In the R-operations, strings are formed from the above formula as follows:

(1)(a) $\quad$ S P ,
(b) $\quad$ S P M_1 ,
(c) $\quad$ S P M_2 ,
(d) $\quad$ S P M_1 M_2 .

Thus, because of the two optional Modifier tagmemes, there are four possible readings from this clause formula.

1.1.2. *P-operations*
In the P-operations, a particular reading, e.g.,

$$+ S \quad + P \quad + M_1$$

---

[1] This formula, which will be modified later on, does not entirely correspond with the formula for the English Active (Transitive) clause set up by Longacre (1968:56). For further discussion on Clause Level procedures, see I ongacre (1968:35 ff.) and Brend (1968: 18–22).

[2] The filler sets have been left out for the sake of brevity.

is permuted in all possible ways. Let us assume that M_1 could occur only in clause initial position or immediately after P. Then only two permutations are possible including the identity permutation (the string identical with the reading rule), namely:

(2)(a) $+ S \ + P \ + M_1$,
  (b) $+ M_1 + S \ + P$.

1.1.3. *E-operations*
The E-operation replaces the function symbols, e.g. S, P, M, with representatives from the sets of fillers, e.g., NP, V_{int}, Prep. Phr.

1.2. Phrase Level analysis
The above operations are now carried out at the Phrase Level. Let us assume that the first Clause Level tagmeme was filled by a noun phrase. This noun phrase may consist of the following Phrase Level tagmemes:

$$+ D \ \pm Sb \ + H ,$$

where D stands for Determiner, Sb for Subjunct and H for Head. [3] A construction which would fit the above formula would be

The cheerful hippopotamus.

1.3. Fillers
The sets of fillers for each tagmeme vary considerably. Some tagmemes in a clause construction could have as their fillers morphemes, noun phrases and even clauses. For instance, the Subject tagmeme in the clause type mentioned above may be filled in the following way:

$+ S : pn/...$

He consumed the rolls.

$+ S : .../n.phr./...$

The repulsive little boy consumed the rolls.

$+ S : .../cl/...$

Whoever broke in through the window consumed the rolls.

---

[3] For a more detailed discussion of Phrase Level analysis see ch. 9.

1.4. Levels and functions

At each level of analysis, we find tagmemes with different functions. Some of the main levels in a tagmemic syntactic analysis would be: Word Level, Phrase Level, Clause Level and Sentence Level. This hierarchy could be further extended if one so desired to include levels above the sentence. In this investigation, particular emphasis will be placed on the Clause Level, although certain concepts of Grammatical Meaning at Phrase Level will also be discussed.

1.5. Tagmemic model developed by Becker

In addition to the two components of a tagmemic unit as discussed earlier, Becker (1967:2) sees the tagmeme as a unit with four basic aspects.

1.5.1. *Grammatical Form*

For instance, in the construction

The little boy walked to the store to get his mother some butter,

Becker (1967:3) argues that four types of information can be supplied about the subject. He says that firstly a grammatical description will give the information that the string *the little boy* has a grammatical relation to the rest of the construction (or some part of it) which can be defined in some way as Subject of the construction.

1.5.2. *Grammatical Meaning*

Secondly, the little boy can be identified as the Actor or Agent (the one who walked). Becker asserts that this information is not identical to the information about the grammatical subject as can be seen by the following examples where the Subject is not an Agent:

Walking is good for you,
The butter is wrapped in aluminium foil.

He claims that it is necessary to supply the information whether X is an Agent, Action, Location, Goal or any one of a number of categories of this sort (Becker 1967:4). In this, he agrees with Fillmore (1968a) who makes this aspect central to his grammatical description.

1.5.3. *Lexical Form*

Thirdly, *the little boy* can be identified as a noun phrase. This information is not derivable from the fact that *the little boy* has been identified as Subject or Agent. The type of filler, although it may at times be tied up with the two previously mentioned aspects, can be ascertained independently from them and must be considered as a third aspect. The italicized examples 1 to 3 are all noun phrases but only in example 1 has the noun phrase the grammatical form of Subject and the grammatical meaning of Agent. On the other hand in example 4, the italicized filler of the subject tagmeme is not a noun phrase.

(1)   *The friendly crocodile* swallowed the fat hunter,
(2)   *My kind old neighbour* was poisoned by mushrooms,
(3)   She scrubbed *the front door steps,*
(4)   *Eating pickled walnuts* is enjoyed by everyone.

1.5.4. *Lexical Meaning*
The fourth aspect that needs to be considered is the information concerning the meaning components of the filler itself. Becker (1967:5) mentions this aspect only briefly and has not given it much consideration in his discussion. He would consider such information as: single, male, human to fall into this category.

1.5.5. *Model showing different aspects of the tagmemic unit*
Becker's four aspects are presented in the following model which was suggested to him by Pike.

	Grammar	Lexicon
Form	A (e.g. Subject)	C (e.g. Noun Phrase)
Meaning	B (e.g. Agent)	D (e.g. single, male, human, etc.)

Aspects of Grammatical Unit

As Becker concentrates in his investigation on the Subject tagmeme, there is little evidence of how he would have dealt with the whole clause construction. Interpreting his suggestion one could, however, assume that his version referring to the previously mentioned example would have been the following:

$$+ S_{ag} \qquad\qquad + P_{act} \qquad\qquad + O_{goal}$$

(Subject-as-Agent   Predicate-as-Action   Object-as-Goal)

Semantic considerations of the kind Object-as-Goal are evident in a number of tagmemic writings before Becker's work — but in all these the syntactic—semantic component (Grammatical Meaning), e.g., Goal, has not been considered as an independent aspect from the Grammatical Form, e.g., Object. It would seem to me that there is a difference between a mere sub-classification of tagmemes (e.g., Subject tagmemes) using as classificatory criteria certain meaning components and an investigation into relationships between these components of Grammatical Meaning somewhat independently of components of Grammatical Form. I feel that Becker is aiming, to some extent, at the latter approach although his pre-occupation with the Subject tagmeme prevents his from fully developing it.

1.6. Two approaches to the establishment of syntactic relations at Clause Level

At this point, it becomes necessary to show a certain departure from the conventional tagmemic approach and to discuss briefly my concept of deep structure relations, which brings me closer into line with an approach suggested by Fillmore (1968a).

1.6.1. *Tagmemes of equal status*

To establish syntactic relations on the Clause Level, one could envisage two main approaches. Firstly, one could consider an approach where the elements are in mutual relation to one another — where there is no specific centre apparent. It is felt that this is, to some extent, the approach chosen by Becker. The Predicate tagmeme, though of importance in his discussions, appears to be more or less of equal status to his Subject tagmeme. This is shown (Becker 1967: ch.3) by the fact that he often obtains the Grammatical Meaning of the Subject tagmeme by reference to fillers only rather than by its relation to the Predicate. [4]

1.6.2. *Predicate centred approach*

The second approach shows an uneven relationship by singling out one element as central. Then relations can be established between the other elements and this central one. For some time, German linguists have favoured

[4] And yet there is evidence that many linguists using a tagmemic method consider the Predicate tagmeme an important and essential factor in Clause Level analysis. Brend (1968: 20), states: 'A clause for the purpose of this analysis, is defined as a grammatical *unit of predication* consisting of one obligatory predicate tagmeme which may be accompanied by other nuclear or peripheral tagmemes'.

this approach, considering the verb as the central element of the clause construction (Satz). Boost (1955:31) acknowledges this fact when, in a discussion on the Predicate he states: 'Die Überlegenheit des Prädikats gegenüber den anderen Satzgliedern, dem Subject, dem Object und der adverbialen Bestimmung, liegt darin, dass es diesen dreien als einzige Bezugsmöglichkeit gegenübersteht'. When referring specifically to German syntax, Drach (1939:69) remarks: 'Als erstes Hauptmerkmal des deutschen Satzbaues fiel die besondere Bedautung auf, die im Satzbauplan dem Verb zukommt. Von dieser Achse aus ordnet sich alles übrige.' Erben (1968:148) makes a similar comment: 'Grundglied der Hierarchie des deutschen Satzes ist das finite Verb ... es ist gewissermassen der eigentliche Träger der aussagenden Bestimmung (Prädikation) der der vom Sprecher eingesetzte 'Organisator' des Bestimmungskomplexes.'

But such observations have been made not only with regard to German syntax. Tesnière (1966:103 ff.) dismisses the traditional Subject—Predicate division as he does not consider that linguistic facts support such a binary cut which does not bring out clearly enough certain parallels that exist between Subject and Object. With him, the verb is central and the subject complementary to it.

Fillmore, by assigning the functions Subject and Object to surface structure only thus frees himself, to some extent, from the methodological restrictions of a Chomsky *Aspects* type grammar and is able to develop his system of Deep Structure Cases where the 'propositional nucleus of sentences in all languages consists of a V and one or more NPs each having a separate case relationship to the P (and hence to the V)' (Fillmore 1968a:51).

1.7. Outline of method and aims

In the present investigation, I wish to apply the second approach using as a starting point Becker's model (see section 1.5.5), but I wish to go beyond Becker's application of it to an analysis of Grammatical Meanings and their co-occurrence with grammatical forms at Clause Level. Certain observations about the Grammatical Meanings of Phrase Level tagmemes have also been included. My approach will thus come close to Fillmore's hypothesis about Deep Structure Cases but whilst agreeing in general with Fillmore than the Cases are implied by each particular verb or adjective I reject the view which seems to be held by Fillmore that adjectives are a subclass of verbal. I would rather claim that any predication, whether expressed by a verb, adjective or noun, implies certain Deep Structure Case or Grammatical Meaning relationships of the other co-occurring elements.

Basically then, the aim of this work is to investigate Grammatical Meanings within a tagmemic framework, to investigate the kinds of relationships implied by various Predicate fillers and to show the extremely variant nature of the occurrence possibilities of the Grammatical Meanings established.

2. BECKER's ASPECT B AND FILLMORE's CASES

2.1. Some weaknesses of the Becker model

In the previous chapter, it was claimed that with his revised model of the tagmeme, Becker had moved beyond the accepted practice of mere subcategorization of the tagmeme practised by most tagmemicists up to then and that he had given himself a tool with which to approach Grammatical Meaning (GM) relationships independently from surface structure considerations and to show their complex interrelation with surface structure forms. Unfortunately, Becker has not made full use of these possibilities. Some of the main weaknesses of his work will be discussed in this chapter.

2.1.1. *Becker's Grammatical Meanings for the Subject tagmeme*

Becker (1967:79−81) establishes the following GMs that can be part of a Subject tagmeme:

(1) Subject as Agent (S_{ag}):
      (1) John runs in the park every morning,
      (2) Whoever was in the room killed Bill,
      (3) One of them came.
(2) Subject as Proposition (S_{prop}):
      (4) The idea that John is frightened amuses me,
      (5) The idea amuses me,
      (6) That John is frightened never occurred to me,
      (7) There is no doubt that John is frightened.
(3) Subject as Instrument (S_{in}):
      (8) A stone struck Bill,
      (9) The key opened the door,
      (10) His left hand brushed away the crumbs,
      (11) His superior intellect won the game.

(4) Subject as Goal (S_{gl}):

    (12) The book burned,

    (13) The book was burned by John,

    (14) Bill was hit by John,

    (15) The tree grew,

    (16) The grass smells fresh,

    (17) The typewriter works fine.

(5) Subject as Time (S_{tm}):

    (18) 1957 was a vintage year,

    (19) The morning is the best time for swimming,

    (20) Sunday passed quickly.

(6) Subject as Location (S_{loc}):

    (21) From here to there is about ten miles,

    (22) Ann Arbor is a nice place to live,

    (23) The south side is warmer,

    (24) It is warmer on the south side,

    (25) There are many houses on the south side.

(7) Subject as Quality (S_{qual}):

    (26) Kindness killed the cat,

    (27) Sincerity may frighten the boy,

    (28) His eagerness to please is embarrassing,

    (29) His anxiety for news overcame his timidity,

    (30) The possibility of finishing seems remote.

(8) Subject as Nexus (S_{nex}):

    (31) For John to be frightened is ridiculous,

    (32) It is ridiculous for John to be frightened,

    (33) Even to begin is to fail.

(9) Subject as State (S_{st}):

    (34) Being cold is no fun,

    (35) His being there made no difference,

    (36) Our being married at home bothered my mother.

(10) Subject as Act (S_{act})

    (37) Playing tennis is fun,

    (38) Constructing the building took all summer,

    (39) The construction of the building took all summer,

    (40) John's love of sports is obsessive,

    (41) Your plan to start in September failed to get support.

(11) Subject as Motion (S_{mo}):

    (42) Walking is healthy,

    (43) Dancing with Mary is a privilege,

    (44) Running five miles a day strengthens the heart.

Instead of basing the definitions of his GMs consistently on the semantic relation of the various tagmemes to the Predicate tagmeme, Becker appears to use different types of criteria for some GMs than he does for others. Because of this rather uneven basis, he creates complications which become particularly apparent when such matters as conjoining are discussed.

2.1.1.1. *Agent, Instrument, Goal.*   Agent, Instrument and Goal appear to be arrived at from a semantic relation between the Subject tagmeme and the Predicate tagmeme, e.g.,

> Whoever was in the room killed Bill.

The X who did the killing can generally be considered as the willing perpetrator of the crime. The GM of Instrument (that is the action was done *with* X) can be defined not only semantically but also by its transform potential:

> The key opened the door,
> The door was opened with the key.

The GM of Goal appears to be unsatisfactorily defined. It suggests that X is the goal towards which the action is directed. The relation between *grew* and *the tree* can hardly be included in this category. In the example

> The typewriter works fine,

it would be dubious whether *typewriter* could be considered as Goal. It would seem rather Instrument.

2.1.1.2. *Proposition, Nexus, State.*   The GMs of Proposition, Nexus and State appear to have been established mainly on the basis of the *form* of the filler (Becker's aspect C). The only set of exponents for the Subject tagmeme with the GM Nexus appears to consist of infinitive constructions (Becker 1967: 117, 4.3.8), whereas the only set of exponents for the Subject tagmeme with the GM of State appears to be a certain type of Predicate clause (e.g., *being cold*). Such a definition based on filler form only is extremely unsatisfactory. No change occurs in the semantic relationship between the Subject tagmeme and the Predicate tagmeme if instead of

> *Being cold* (is no fun),

to be cold were to be substituted. The same would hold if these GMs were to appear in Object tagmemes, e.g.,

>   Joe likes eating pickled gherkins,
>   Joe likes to eat pickled gherkins.

In addition to filler form criteria, the GM Proposition appears also to be defined by certain meaning components (Becker's aspect D). The set of exponents appears to consist of a subset of Proposition clauses (*that* clauses) and a subset of Phrases with a Proposition Head (Becker 1967:115, 4.3.2). The nature of the Proposition Head is not very clearly defined. Becker's examples of Proposition Heads are: act, idea, notion, etc.

2.1.1.3. *Quality.*   One of Becker's GMs which relies heavily on the meaning of the filler is Quality. The Heads of the phrase constructions are, with one exception [1] nouns denoting quality (Becker 1967:117, 4.3.7). If one applied a semantic relation criterion to Becker's example

>   Kindness killed the cat,

one would rather be inclined to define the GM of the Subject tagmeme as Instrument, e.g.,

>   The cat was killed *with kindness.*

2.1.1.4. *Time, Location.*   Filler meaning combined with transform potential appears to be used for the GMs Time and Location. The set of exponents for the Subject tagmeme with the GM Time consists of three subsets (Becker 1967:116):
(a) the subset: Phrase with a Time Head:

>   The morning (is the time to go);

(b) the subset: Relative Phrase (time relator—axis [2] prepositional phrase):

>   From June to September (is the time to go);

---

[1] It is puzzling that the noun 'possibility' in the example 'The possibility of finishing seems remote' should have been included by Becker under GM Quality Heads.

[2] A relator tagmeme on the Phrase Level has the function of relating the following sequence (the axis) to the clause or phrase in which the axis is embedded.

(c) the subset: Relative clause (wh-time clause):

> Whenever John is ready (is the time to go).

The set of exponents for the Subject tagmeme with the GM Location also consists of three subsets (Becker 1967:116):
(a) the subset: Phrase with a Location Head:

> Chicago (is too far);

(b) the subset: Relative Phrase (location relator–axis prepositional phrase):

> From here to Chicago (is too far);

(c) the subset: Relative Clause (wh-location clause):

> Wherever John is staying (is too far).

I do not consider the definition of GM by the head of the phrase construction a convincing criterion. The subset of phrases with Location Head mentioned under the GM Location above should also have been included under the GM Goal. See example:

> The book burned. [3]

One could just as well say

> Chicago burned.

Similarly

> The book was burned by John,
> Chicago was burned by the mob. [4]

2.1.1.5. *Act, Motion.*   The meaning of the filler head appears to have been used as the main criterion for GM as Act and as Motion. Even if we accept this criterion we cannot agree with Becker's distinction between Act and

---

[3] See section 2.1.1.1, example (4)(12).
[4] See section 2.1.1.1, example (4)(13).

Motion. It appears that Act refers to an action and Motion to a movement which, however, need not be in a horizontal direction. We cannot distinguish clearly between *playing tennis* (Becker's GM as Act) and *dancing with Mary* (Becker's GM as Motion). That the border between these two GMs is vague can be shown by using Becker's own criterion of conjoining. [5] Contrary to Becker's statements, these two are freely conjoinable, e.g.,

> Playing tennis and dancing with Mary are fun.

2.1.2. *Becker's criterion of conjoining*

In his discussions of Longacre's method, Becker (1967:58) criticizes his formula which makes it possible for any tagmeme to be optionally repeated if so indicated. Becker states that repeating a tagmeme in a reading rule is equivalent to conjoining, for if a tagmeme is actually repeated then, at least in English, a conjunction marker (*and, but, or,* and others, including special intonation) is obligatory, e.g.,

> John fishes with a fly rod,
>
> + S   + P   + M

if $+ S^2$ is read we may get

> John and Bill fish with a fly rod.

Becker claims that this is not a sufficiently precise rule to include all of the constraints on conjoining, even with *and*. He sees the reason for this in the fact that Longacre's reading-rules provide only information about the Grammatical Form of the tagmeme and not about the GM. The following construction would be considered unacceptable in standard English:

> * John and a stone hit Bill.

Becker sees the reason for the non-conjoinability of the two Subject tagmemes in the above example in the fact that although their Grammatical Form is identical, namely Subject, their GMs differ. That of *John* is Agent, that of *the stone* is Instrument and he asserts that tagmemes may be conjoined only if they have the same Grammatical Form *and* the same GM.

---

[5] See section 2.1.2 for further discussion on this point.

2.1.2.1.   This rule is basically sound. However, as discussed above, the criteria Becker uses for establishing his GMs are not always consistent and thus his own conjoining rule is at times inapplicable. For example, as already stated earlier (section 2.1.1) if we take from Becker's list a Subject classified as Subject as Act and a Subject classified as Subject as Motion, we can obtain

> Playing tennis and dancing with Mary are fun.

Or again, we may take an example from Subject as State

> Being cold is no fun.

This Subject will also conjoin with Subject as Act to give

> Being cold and playing tennis are no fun.

Against this, we may *not* conjoin the Subjects of some of the examples, e.g., Subject as Location

> From here to there   and   Ann Arbor,

to give

> From here to there and Ann Arbor (are pleasant areas).

Or again, let us try to conjoin some of the Subjects under Subject as Act:

> Constructing the building,

and

> The construction of the building.

To be fair, we should change *building* to two different types of building:

> Constructing the hall and the construction of
> the shed took all summer.

2.1.3. *Need for unified criterion for the establishment of Grammatical Meanings*
There is no doubt that in a closely knit unit such as the tagmeme, the four

aspects (Grammatical Form, Grammatical Meaning, Lexical Form, Lexical Meaning) do exert an influence on one another. I wish to assert, however, that in an attempt to establish aspect B (Grammatical Meaning) a unified criterion must be used and that this could only be the underlying semantic relationship between the tagmemes in a construction which is based on the Predicate tagmeme as the central point of reference.

This in no way minimizes the importance of aspects C and D. Aspect C can play an important part in the conjoinability of tagmemes, as has been shown above. [6] Aspect D often causes variations in the degree of acceptability (particularly in everyday language):

> Joe built a water,
> Joe opened the door with a fish.

2.2. Fillmore's concept of Deep Structure Case

Fillmore (1968a:3) states that his paper 'will plead that the grammatical notion Case deserves a place in the base component of the grammar of every language'. He continues: 'what is needed is a conception of base structure in which case relationships are primitive terms of the theory and in which such concepts as 'subject' and 'direct object' are missing. The latter are regarded as proper only to the surface structure of some (but possibly not all) languages.'

Fillmore's use of the term Case would seem, in general, to accord with Becker's use of the term Grammatical Meaning but the latter term is preferable because Case has been used for so long to designate Surface Structure manifestations such as Accusative and Dative affixation in Latin. Fillmore (1968a: 19 ff.) pleads a case for the retention of the term Case but we shall prefer Grammatical Meaning and use the term Case only in discussion of Fillmore's work or in reference to surface phenomena.

We might object, too, to Fillmore's use of 'only'. This seems to suggest that Surface Structure is, in some way, of lesser importance or lesser interest than deep structure. It is of considerable interest to the linguist to learn whether certain GM relationships are or are not overtly marked in a particular language, whether two (or more) verbs with the same GM implications may or may not have complete congruity in surface manifestations in a particular language and whether the same surface manifestation is used for two different GMs as is the case in Pitjantjatjara where one affixed morpheme stands for Instrumental and Locative and where another affixed morpheme stands for Benefactive and Purposive as well as being a reduced form of a Directional.

---

[6] E.g., constructing the hall and the construction of the shed, see section 2.1.2.1.

2.2.1. *Covert categories*

Fillmore (1968a:3) continues: 'Two assumptions are essential to the development of the argument, assumptions that are, in fact, taken for granted by workers in the generative grammar tradition. The first of these is *the centrality of syntax*.' His second assumption is 'the importance of covert categories' and he continues: 'Many recent and not-so-recent studies have convinced us of the relevance of grammatical properties lacking obvious 'morphemic' realizations but having a reality that can be observed on the basis of selectional constraints and transformational possibilities. We are constantly finding that grammatical features found in one language show up in some form or other in other languages as well, if we have the subtlety it takes to discover the covert categories.'

I am in general agreement with this second assumption but it needs to be stressed that a linguist working along these lines may be misled by 'selectional constraints and transformational possibilities'. There is a danger of seeing general transformational relationships where they are not really so general. Thus if we pair Fillmore's (1968a:25) examples 37 and 38

Chicago is windy,
It is windy in Chicago,

and continue with a great number of similar pairs, making Chicago dirty, noisy, unpleasant, delightful, glorious and so on we may come to the conclusion that Chicago is always Locative. However, when we make Chicago important, medium sized or distant we may produce some queer transformations:

It is important in Chicago,
It is medium sized in Chicago,
It is nearby in Chicago.

These are sentences which we can meaningfully interpret, but they are not transformationally related to

Chicago is important,
Chicago is medium sized,
Chicago is nearby.

However, we can agree with Fillmore (1968a:5) when he suggests: 'that there are many semantically relevant syntactic relationships involving nouns and the structures that contain them, that these relationships [...] are in

large part covert but are nevertheless empirically discoverable, that they form
a specific finite set, and that observations made about them will turn out to
have considerable cross-linguistic validity.'

2.3. An examination of Fillmore's Cases
In fitting his views on Deep Structure Case into a generative—transformational framework, Fillmore (1968a:23) suggests the following:
' In the basic structure of sentences, then, we find what might be called the
'proposition', a tenseless set of relationships involving verbs and nouns (and
embedded sentences, if there are any), separated from what might be called
the 'modality' constituent. This latter will include such modalities on the
sentence-as-a-whole as negation, tense, mood, and aspect. The exact nature
of the modality constituent may be ignored for our purposes. It is likely,
however, that certain 'cases' will be directly related to the modality constituent as others are related to the proposition itself, as for example certain temporal adverbs.'
The first base rule, then is 28, abbreviated to 28'.

(28)   Sentence → Modality + Proposition,
(28')   S → M + P.

The P constituent is 'expanded' as a verb and one or more case categories.
A later rule will automatically provide for each of the cases the categorial
realization as NP (except for one which may be an embedded S). In effect
the case relations are represented by means of dominating category symbols.
The expansion of P may be thought of as a list of formulas of the form
seen in 29, where *at least one case category must be chosen and where no
case category appears more than once* (the italics are mine).

(29) $P + V + C_1 + ... C_n$.

To adapt this to tagmemic theory, we could state that each verb implies
an array of GMs and that each clause must contain at Clause Level at least
one GM, no GM occurring more than once at Clause Level within a clause.
The tagmemic distinction of levels simplifies our problem in that we can
concentrate our attention upon GM at the Clause Level, but, as will be discussed later, there are GM relationships at the Phrase and Word Levels as well.
The above rule may need further modification in several respect — notably
in the occurrences of GMs with BE and HAVE.

2.3.1. *Cases established by Fillmore*

Fillmore (1968a:24) has discussed a number of cases in greater detail and has made suggestions regarding two others. Those of which he appears to be certain are as follows (the italics are mine):

Agentive (A), the Case of the *typically animate perceived* instigator of the action identified by the verb.

Instrumental (I), the case of the *inanimate* force or object causally involved in the action or state identified by the verb.

Dative (D), the Case of the *animate* being affected by the state or action identified by the verb.

Factitive (F), the Case of the object or being resulting from the action or state identified by the verb, or understood as a part of the meaning of the verb.

Locative (L), the Case which identifies *the lcoation or spatial orientation of the state or action identified by the verb.*

Objective (O), the semantically most neutral Case, the Case of anything representable by a noun whose role in the action or state identified by the verb is identified by the semantic interpretation of the verb itself; conceivably the concept should be limited to things which are affected by the action or state identified by the verb. The term is not to be confused with the notion of Direct Object, nor with the name of the Surface Case synonymous with accusative.

Before considering the two other Cases suggested by Fillmore, and before ourselves suggesting any extra Cases or GMs, it is necessary to discuss the previously listed Cases one by one, particularly in regard to the italicized words or phrases.

2.3.2. *Agentive* (A)

The word *perceived* merits consideration. Perceived by whom? We could understand this as "perceived" by the speaker/writer and ideal listener/reader.

From a linguistic universals viewpoint, it would seem that *perceived* may be different for different languages and cultures. In an example like

The sea washed away the shore,

it would seem that speakers of language A could take *the sea* as an Agent and this would be shown overtly in the surface structure, e.g., by affixation to the word for *sea* or by a particular subclassification of nominals to which *sea* would belong together with those representing animate (or perhaps even human) beings.

On the other hand, speakers of language B might also consider *sea* as an Agent, but there may be no overt distinction as in A.

Again, speakers of language C could take *sea* as an Instrument, and there would be overt marking such that *sea* would belong to the same class of nominals as, e.g., knife, spear, axe.

Finally, speakers of language D, whilst equally considering *sea* as an Instrument would have no overt surface marking.

The following matrix may illustrate this:

	Speakers consider *sea* as Agent	Speakers consider *sea* as Instrument
Overt distinction, e.g., affix or nominal subclassification	A	C
No overt distinction	B	D

This matrix is, of course, a simplification as in each language group there are likely to be speakers who would consider *sea, wind,* etc., as Agents whilst others would consider them as Instruments. Again, any one speaker may consider the *sea* or *wind* as more of an Agent on one occasion or more of an Instrument on another.

Thus, we would consider *the sea* in

The sea claimed many lives,

as more obviously an Agent than in

The sea washed away the shore,

and even this would seem to be more an Agent than in

The sea has damaged the sea wall.

It is quite apparent that what we are considering are mostly what, in legal language, are referred to as "Acts of God". One could well take the sea, wind, lightning and other natural forces as Instruments of God and this would be appropriate in certain cultures. On the other hand, there are powers which, in themselves, seem to have Godlike qualities in other cultures, or at least animate qualities. Thus in Kukata [7] the utterance: /wal^{y}pa waŋkin^y/ 'the wind speaks' is quite normal in reference to the sound of the wind. In English it is semi-poetic and yet 'The wind is howling' is less so, as is 'The wind is battering the door'.

The other point is *typically animate.* Fillmore does have a footnote in reference to this: 'The escape qualification 'typically' expresses my awareness that contexts which I will say require agents are sometimes occupied by 'inaminate' nouns like *robot* or 'human institution' nouns like *nation*' (1968a: 24, fn. 31). Since I know of no way of dealing with these matters at the moment, I shall just assume for all Agents that they are animate'.

However, it is not only a matter of robots or 'human institutions'. It is quite obvious that: *wind, sea, river,* etc., may be included within animate. In English, they are on a borderline. The sea may: *speak, destroy, eat* (at the shore), *rage, howl, claim* (victims), *murder, lap* (shores) but, of course it does not *stand, walk, fly.* (Neither, though, do many definitely animate beings, e.g., snakes.)

There are, however, other things which, at least in a western-type culture, we take as inanimate and without minds and wills of their own. These include planes, cars, trains and all kinds of machines.

Fillmore suggests that these are Instrumental and argues from the examples of

(23)   The car broke the window with its fender,

(25)   The car's fender broke the window.

He has explained that

(22)   *A hammer broke the glass with a chisel,

'is unacceptable, in particular, on the interpretation that both *hammer* and *chisel* are understood instrumentally. It cannot represent a sentence containing an Agent and an Instrument, since the noun *hammer* is inanimate' (Fillmore 1968a:22).

Therefore

(24)   *The car broke the window with a fender,

is unacceptable. However, 'Sentences 23 and 25 are agentless sentences con-

---

[7] An Australian aboriginal dialect of the Western Desert, related to Pitjantjatjara. The example is included in material recorded by the writer.

taining *a possessed noun* as the Instrument (*the car's fender*). The rules for choosing a subject allow an option in this case: either the entire instrument phrase may appear as the subject (as in 25), or the 'possessor' alone may be made the subject, the remainder of the instrument phrase appearing with the preposition *with* (as in 23). The second option requires that a 'trace' be left behind in the instrument phrase, in the form of the appropriate possessive pronoun' (Fillmore, 1968a:23).

Against this argument, let us consider such examples as

> This machine polishes the floor with a rotary brush,
> This excavator digs out the earth with a large scoop.

Examples such as

> This machine polishes the floor with its rotary brush,
> This excavator digs out the earth with its large scoop,

are also perfectly acceptable.

The clue to this problem seems to be the one suggested elsewhere by Fillmore (1968a:22): the distinction between *Alienable* and *Inalienable* Possession.

Inalienably possessed Instruments are almost always indicated in English with a possessive, e.g.,

> He hit the table with his hand,
> He tripped Bill with his foot.

The exceptions are stock expressions, especially where what is possessed is qualified, e.g.,

> He wiped a weary hand across his brow,
> He cast an eye (or a careful eye) over the document.

In fact, in such examples, there is a suggestion of a separate Instrument.

The *car's fender* falls into the class of Inalienable Possession. It is as inalienably possessed as *hand* or *foot*. These may be lost by accident but all are integral parts of the car or human.

Alienable Possessions, on the other hand, do not need possessive indication — it is optional except insofar as it is necessary to indicate whose Instrument is used. Thus

> He hit the nail with a/his hammer,
> This machine polishes the floor with a/its rotary brush.

One could imagine also such examples as

> This machine polishes the floor quite well with
> your machine's rotary brush.

If we do not use the possessive in such cases it is because we feel that the rotary brush or whatever it is is detachable from the machine or is, at least, in some way distinct. Notice that:

> This car hit the lamp post with that car's fender,

sound like something from a cartoon film.

Thus we could amend Fillmore's description by changing *typically animate* to *typically animate (except in the case of natural forces or mechanical devices)*.

2.3.3. *Instrumental* (I)

Fillmore (1968a:23, fn. 32) has, himself, pointed out the example of

> I rapped him on the head with a snake.

This rather outlandish example of an animate Instrument could be backed by such examples as

> They use oxen to thresh the grain,
> He got the bird with a falcon,
> He caught the rabbits with a ferret,
> He conquered the country with tanks, planes and a big army.

In the final example, the *army* is as much an Instrument as the *tanks* and the *planes.* To the objection that an army, as such, is not animate, we could substitute *ten thousand men.*

Fillmore (1968a:23, fn. 32) has suggested that the underlying structure of *a snake* in the example he cites is something equivalent to *the body of a snake.* This would work, but more than the body of a ferret is needed for catching rabbits.

It might be argued that we would need another Case or Grammatical Meaning but surely animate beings are used by others as Instruments.

In an example such as

Ten thousand men conquered the country,

it might be difficult to decide whether the *ten thousand men* should be considered as Agentive or Instrumental. Information outside the clause could give a clue but otherwise it is ambiguous.

2.3.4. *Dative* (D)

Here again, we need to modify *animate* to *usually* or *typically animate.* This is not because of examples such as

I gave the car some petrol.

It might be objected here that *car* is Locative and that the example is equivalent to

I put some petrol into the car,

whereas

I gave Jim a biscuit,

is not equivalent to

I put a biscuit into Jim.

It is simply that it is necessary to cover examples such as

He endowed his school with a scholarship,
Tom gave the hospital fund a cheque for $1,000.

We know that the scholarship was endowed through some human recipient and that the school is an institution of human beings. We know, too, that the hospital fund is a buman institution and that the money was probably handed or sent to a secretary.

Actually, in the second example, if we were to delete *a cheque,* we could have

Tom put $1,000 into the hospital fund,

but the introduction of *a cheque* makes

Tom put a cheque for $1,000 into the hospital fund,

unlikely. Also

*He put a scholarship into his school,

is impossible.

Obviously, we are dealing here with examples on the borderline between an inanimate building, fund, etc., and the humans who are connected with them.

2.3.5. *Factitive* (F)

Fillmore's definition here seems quite adequate and satisfactory. Interestingly, the Factitive within the verb is clearly shown in Pitjantjatjara in such examples as

watiŋku wilt^{y}ani　　　　　'The man makes a wurley'
　　　　　　　　　　　　　　　　　(rough shelter) ,

where $wilt^ya$ = 'wurley' and *-ni* is the Present Tense affixation. The affix *-ŋku* to *wati-* is an overt Agentive affixation. Another example is:

watiŋku t^{y}ukurmanan^{y}i　　　'The man dreams',

where t^yukur = 'a dream'.

We may consider that in an example such as

He has become an old man,

an old man is a noun phrase in the Factitive Case or with a Factitive GM. Similarly in:

He has aged,

the verb *aged* includes the Factitive. In an example, too, such as

They season the timber,

it is the verb *season* which includes the Factitive case or GM and not the *timber*. After all, the timber *was* timber before the seasoning process. In an example such as:

> They make the timber into furniture,

it is *into furniture* which is Factitive. It was not furniture before the making.

2.3.6. *Locative* (L)

This will be particularly considered in ch. 3 but it may be mentioned here that there is a difference between Location of a state and Location of an action.

2.3.7. *Objective* (C)

Here, Fillmore seems to be unsure. We are first told that this is 'the case of anything representable by a noun whose role in the action or state identified by the verb is identified by the semantic interpretation of the verb itself'. This is a rather vague definition but we are then told: 'conceivably the concept should be limited to things where are *affected* by the action or state identified by the verb' (the italics are mine).

It is therefore necessary to investigate what Fillmore considers as being in the Objective Case and with what verbs these instances of the Objective Case occur. The following is the complete list from 'The case for case'. Wherever possible, Fillmore's 'case frames' and examples are given but otherwise my examples are given to illustrate. In each case, the page reference is given, and the Objective Case element is italicized:

p.27	remove	[—— O + A]	Joe removed *the book.*
p.27	open	[—— O + A]	Joe opened *the door.*
p.27	give	[—— O + D + A]	Joe gave Mary *the book.*
p.29	cook	[—— O(A)]	Mother is cooking *the potatoes.*
p.30	see	[—— O + D]	Joe saw *the film.*
p.30	show	[—— O + D + A]	Joe showed Fred *the books.*
p.30	like	[—— O + D]	Joe likes *chutney.*
p.30	please	[—— O + D]	*Chutney* pleases Joe.
p.31	know	[—— O + D]	Joe knows *Fred.*
p.31	look	[—— O + A]	Joe looks *at the film.*
p.31	learn	[—— O + A]	Joe learnt *the lesson.*
p.31	hear	[—— O + D]	Joe heard *a sound.*
p.31	listen	[—— O + A]	Joe listened *to the music.*

Let us consider which of the italicized phrases represents anything affected by the action or state identified by the verb. The only definite ones are those occurring with the verbs *remove, open, cook*. Those which are definitely *not* affected are those occurring with *see, like, please, know, look, learn, hear, listen.*

Notice that with *remove, open, cook* we can use Fillmore's (1968a:4) 'affectum—effectum' test and produce:

> What Joe did to the book was remove it,
> What Joe did to the door was open it,
> What mother does with the potatoes is cook them.

However, we cannot have

> What Joe did to the film was see it,
> What Joe does to the lesson is learn it,

and so on. What about: *give, show*? If we try this test, we can obtain

> What Joe did to the book was give it to Mary,
> What Joe did to the books was show them to Fred.

Most listeners would probably accept the first of this pair and many would accept the second. However, it is doubtful whether the parallel transformations of

> Joe gave a block of land to his daughter,
> Joe showed Mary the city sights,

would be acceptable, thus

> What Joe did to a block of land was give it to his daughter,
> What Joe did to the city sights was show them to Mary.

The difference is obvious. The book may be physically handed to Mary when it is given. The books may be physically handed to Fred when they are shown. But the block of land and the city sights are hardly *handed*. In fact they are in no way affected.

Thus it would seem that instead of an Objective Case or GM, it may be necessary to have two Cases or GMs, one for whatever is completely unaffected and one for what is affected. We shall return to this problem later.

3. SOME PROBLEMS OF LOCATION

3.0. Problems of Location

There are a number of problems connected with Location. Some of these have been raised by Fillmore but there are others which merit consideration. Briefly these are the problems associated with:
(1) the difference between:

    (i)   John keeps his car in the garage,

and

    (ii)   John washes his car in the garage, (Fillmore 1968a:26, fn. 34);

(2) the problem of:

        It is hot in the studio / The studio is hot
        (Fillmore 1968a:42–44);

(3) the problem of:

        There are many toys in the box / The box has many toys in it
        (Fillmore 1968a:44–47);

(4) the problem of:

        Mary pinched John's nose / Mary pinched John on the nose
        (Fillmore 1968a:68–74).

To a great extent, these problems are interrelated, but for the purposes of exposition, it will be necessary to keep them apart as far as possible.

3.1. One or two Locatives

Fillmore, in the previously referred to footnote says: 'The putative contrast between locational and directional expressions as well as the distinction between 'optional' and 'obligatory' locative expressions ... seem to point to the difference between elements which are 'inside the VP' and elements which are 'outside the VP'.

(i)   John keeps his car in the garage.
(ii)   John washes his car in the garage.

In our terms this would be equivalent either to determining whether there is a difference between an L as a constituent of P and an L as a constituent of M, or whether there can be two L elements within P, distinguished in terms of degree of selectivity of verbs. The highly restricting L selects verbs like *keep, put,* and *leave,* but not *polish, wash,* and *build;* the weakly restricting L selects verbs like *polish, wash,* and *build,* but not *believe, know,* or *want.*

However this distinction is interpreted, the second or 'outer' L is in some respects similar in its 'selectional' properties to what might be called the *Benefactive case* B. B, too, is involved in the selection of verbs in the sense that some verbs do not accept B modification (*'He is tall for you'); but the restriction here may have more to do with *dependency relations between cases* than with dependencies directly connected with the verb. It appears, in fact, that those verbs which allow 'outer L' and B modifications are precisely those which take Agents. I have no idea how these dependencies can be stated, but it would appear that the second L and the B can appear only in sentences containing A's.'

Fillmore's reference to 'elements which are 'inside the VP' and elements which are 'outside the VP' ' seems to be a reference to an *Aspects* type model. Thus it would seem that Fillmore's outer L is similar to Chomsky's Locatives which are immediately dominated by Predicate while his inner L is similar to Chomsky's Locatives which are immediately dominated by VP.

Reverting to the two examples themselves, it is noticeable that although we can omit the Locative in (ii) to give:

John washes his car,

we cannot omit the Locative in (i) to give:

John keeps his car,

at least, not with the same meaning.

Elsewhere Fillmore (1968a:31) suggests that: 'The transformation which accounts for the 'true imperatives' can apply only to sentences containing A's, and the occurrence of B expressions (and 'outer L's') is dependent on the presence of an A.' There may be some doubt as to whether *John* in:

> John keeps his car in the garage,

is Agentive or not, but it would definitely seem to be so in

> John put his car into the garage.

Here again, the Locative element must occur. It would seem, though that

> Put your car into the garage,

is a true Imperative. We may also have the progressive aspect of the verb, which Fillmore (1968a:31) seems to suggest is a test for Agentive. Of course, although Fillmore states that 'the occurrence of B expressions (and outer L's) is dependent on the presence of an A', he does not explicitly state that the presence of an A implies that any L will be an outer L. In fact this seems patently not to be the case. All the following would seem to have Agentive Subjects and inner L's:

> Joe put the letter into the file,
> Gary threw the ball over the fence,
> Claude sent the parcel to Melbourne.

With all of these, a permutation of the Locative to the beginning of the clause is not normal, except with particular emphasis on the location. Thus

> Into the file Joe put the letter,

is unusual. Furthermore, it is true that certain Prepositions may occur with inner L's and others may not, according to the particular verb.

With outer L's, the selection of Preposition seems to be more determined by the following Noun. Thus

> John washes his car in the garage (in the garden, in the street),
> John washes his car at the service station (at home, at the factory).

Thus given the verb *wash* and the object *car,* the selection of the Preposition is further determined by whether it is *in* the garage, etc., or *at* the service station, etc.

It may be noticed that outer L's are more readily permutable to a position at the beginning of the clause, thus

> In the garage Joe is washing his car.

Note that the progressive form of the verb is more likely with this permutation, but although we can have

> Joe is keeping his car in the garage,

where *keep* implies an inner Locative, the permutation

> In the garage, Joe is keeping his car,

is even less likely than

> In the garage, Joe keeps his car.

We would define an inner Locative as a Locative which is obligatory (as with *put*) and/or directional (as in the case of: *Tom walked to town*). Outer Locatives we would define as Locatives optionally co-occurring with certain predicate fillers and with the Agentive GM, for example: *Mary cooked the meal in the kitchen.*

3.1.1. *Inner, outer and far-outer Locative*

However, there is still the problem of Fillmore's statement that the weakly restricting L, that is the outer L selects verbs like *polish, wash,* and *build* but not *believe, know,* or *want.* Of course, with these, we could certainly have what could be called in tagmemic terms Phrase Level Locatives, e.g., [1]

> Bill believed *the man at the office,*
> Fred knows *the girl in the library,*
> Mary wants *the dress in the shop window.*

---

[1] Phrase Level constructions which serve as fillers of the Object tagmeme at Clause Level are italicized.

In each example here, the Locative phrase specifies the particular item. However, it is true that we do not have such examples as

> In the library, Fred knows the girl,
> Fred knows the girl, in the library,

(in the sense that it is in the library that Fred knows the girl). However, it seems that there is an even more outer Locative as may be exemplified in

> In that town, people know their neighbours.
> In that country, people believe their politicians.
> In that region, the people want a new dam.

This kind of Locative seems to be so outer that it plays no part at all in the selection of verbs or, put differently, any verb may co-occur with it.

Thus it would seem that far outer Locatives may co-occur with any verb, the outer Locatives are optional and may co-occur with many verbs which imply Agentive whilst the inner Locatives co-occur with a more restricted range of verbs and are obligatory, directional or both.

Further criteria for distinguishing the three degrees of location would seem to be:

Inner Locative: The Agent, if any, is not usually located at the Location indicated.

Outer Locative: The Agent is usually located at the Location indicated.

Far Outer Locative: There need be no Agent, it is freely permutable, independently of the other Locatives, to clause beginning or final position.

3.1.2. *Live in, inhabit, occupy, live, dwell, reside*

Related to this problem is the one exemplified by

> Ten people live in that house,
> Joe lives in that house,
> The King lives in the palace,
> The Chinese live in China.

With some of the above, it is possible to substitute *inhabit* for *live in* and also to have a Passive variant. Thus, we can have

> China is inhabited by the Chinese,

but

> The Chinese inhabit China,
> China is lived in by the Chinese,

are dubious.

With our first example, we can have

> Ten people inhabit that house,
> That house is inhabited by ten people,
> That house is lived in by ten people.

With our second example, we cannot have

> *Joe inhabits that house,
> *That house is inhabited by Joe,
> *That house is lived in by Joe.

However, when the dweller is the King, it seems more acceptable to have

> The King inhabits the palace,
> The palace is inhabited by the King,
> The palace is lived in by the King,

and if, instead of the Chinese living in China, we had

> The Ongobongo tribe inhabits that village,

we could also have

> That villaged is inhabited by the Ongobongo tribe,
> That village is lived in by the Ongobongo tribe.

It would seem, therefore, that a race of people may *inhabit* a village, town or country as well as *live in* it. Sometimes, *live in* is fully synonymous with *inhabit* as with the ten people in the house, and then both *inhabit* and *live in* may occur in the Active or Passive. Sometimes, as with the *Chinese* example, the two are not fully synonymous. It would seem that a number of people may *live in* or *inhabit* a house, but one person can *live in* but not *inhabit* a

building unless he be an important personage like a king, where there is probably an implication of his retinue residing there as well.

We may notice that the questions we may ask to receive respectively our
four examples as responses are:

What do the ten people live in?
Where do the ten people live?
What do the ten people inhabit?
Where does Joe live?
What does Joe live in?   (if we expect a response such as:
                           a caravan, a house or a tent),
Where does the King live?
What does the King live in?
What does the King inhabit?
Where do the Chinese live?   (the other two types would only
                              be if we were enquiring about
                              their dwellings),
Where does the Ongobongo tribe live?
What does the Ongobongo tribe live in?
What does the Ongobongo tribe inhabit?

Thus it would seem that we have (at least) a verb *live* and another verb *live in*
or perhaps, preferably, a Predicate filled by *live* and a Predicate filled by
live + in.

In the light of our interrogative examples, it seems dubious whether we can
claim that *inhabit* and *live in* necessarily imply Locative. It may simply be that
these usually take Objects which are filled by Nouns representing Locations,
but we can have

Ants are living in that post,
The eaves are inhabited by starlings,
The old cupboard is lived in by a family of mice.

The conjoining of, for example, *buy* and *live in* seems to support this hypothesis. Thus, we can have

Joe bought and lived in a caravan,

but not

*Joe bought and swam in a pool.

Furthermore, although we can have

> Joe bought a house and lived there,

we do not have

> *Joe bought a caravan and lived there,

but
> Joe bought a caravan and lived in it.

We can therefore see that if *live in, inhabit* – and also *occupy* – do imply the Locative case or GM we shall need other criteria than those already illustrated. We could say, tentatively, that
(a) *live in, inhabit* and *occupy* do not imply Locative but may co-occur with far outer Locatives;
(b) *live, dwell, reside* co-occur with inner Locatives;
(c) *live* (either in the sense of 'be alive' or of 'live it up', 'have a good time') do not imply Locative but may co-occur with far-outer Locatives as in:

> The King lives – in exile,
> Joe is living, up in the big city.

However, there seems to be something intuitively wrong in our statement under (a), above. We know that if a house is *lived in* we are concerned with people occupying a spatial area. The same applies if a house is *occupied* or *inhabited* or if a country is occupied, for example by enemy troops. What is needed is another diagnostic test. Perhaps a more satisfactory one for this type of verb is:
What *location* is V-ed? (where V represents the verb).
Thus we can have, What location is *lived in, inhabited* or *occupied*? The difference between verbs in (a) and (b) then is a matter of the surface structure manifestation of the Locative. In (a) it occurs as Object in Active clauses and as Subject in Passive clauses, whereas in (b) it always occurs as a Locative phrase.

3.2. It is hot in X – X is hot
Fillmore (1968a:42) suggests that 'verbs expressing meteorological conditions have the frame feature + [___ L] '. He goes on to explain that by Subject copying and then by second copy deletion and Subject–Preposition deletion we get sentences like

> The studio is hot.

On the other hand, if the first copy is replaced by its pro form (in this context, *it*), we get sentences like

It is hot in the studio.

However, it is not only a matter of meteorological conditions. The following examples seem to be as much related as the previous examples:

It is pleasant in the studio,
The studio is pleasant,

and also

It is dirty in the studio,
The studio is dirty,

and even

It is roomy in the studio,
The studio is roomy.

However, this relation does not seem to hold with

The studio is medium sized,
*It is medium sized in the studio.

Conversely, we may consider

It is cool in Darwin,

which is not the same as

Darwin is cool,

or

It was wonderful at Joe's place,

which is certainly not the same as

Joe's place was wonderful.

In fact, Joe's place may have been anything but wonderful. Why, then, was *it* wonderful there? Perhaps the clue is that *it* is not just a dummy subject or a pro form for the first copy. Becker (1967:92) has suggested that in the case of his Subject as Proposition, *it* may replace the category word *idea*. He goes on to suggest that: 'We would give a similar interpretation to example (25):

(25)   It is warmer on the south side.

That is, we interpret (25) as a defocussing permutation of

(24)   The south side is warmer,

in both cases the subject is S_{loc} .'

However, he does not say what category word *it* replaces in this case. Obviously, it is not *idea*. We would not consider that *it* replaces a category word *location* either but rather something which might best be expressed as *atmosphere* in its broadest sense. Thus, *it* (the atmosphere) could have been wonderful at Joe's place without Joe's place being at all wonderful. Similarly, the atmosphere could have been (this time in a meteorological sense) cool in Darwin although we would not say that Darwin was cool.

This leads on to the fact that if we say that a particular town or country is *hot, cool, windy,* etc., we mean that these are the prevailing conditions there unless we specify otherwise by some temporal adjunct, e.g.,

Melbourne is windy today.

On the other hand, to say that:

It is windy in Wellington,

is, in itself ambiguous. It may mean that it is windy there today, for example in the context of a weather report, or it may be a generalization, as, for example, in a geography book about New Zealand.

It is true that for certain locations, the 'atmosphere' of the place and a feature of the place may always coincide. Thus, a spacious room might always have a spacious atmosphere but an extremely unpleasant house might, on some particular occasion, have a most pleasant atmosphere in it.

Thus, although we could say that in these pairs of examples there is always a Locative, appearing in the ones as Subject and in the others as Prepositional Phrase, it seems to be an overstatement to claim that they are necessarily transformationally related or that the one is a permutation of the other.

3.3. There are X in Y − Y has X (in it) − X are in Y

Fillmore (1968a:82) claims that 'Under certain conditions, a first copy L may be replaced by an expletive *there*. The case frame [___O+L] may be filled by a blank verb (that is, zero). This situation (of verbless sentences) may call for the introduction of the element *be* into the M constituent, which is a process we have already seen to be necessary for verbs which are adjectives as well as for verbs which have been modified through the addition of the feature passive. For verbless sentences of the type [___O+L], the 'normal' subject choice is O.' Fillmore then shows that by transformations we eventually obtain

Many toys are in the box.

He then suggests that 'An alternative subject choice, through subject copying, is the L' and thus we would obtain

There are many toys in the box.

Finally, 'An alternative to replacing the first copy L by expletive *there* is to retain the L NP as subject. This decision requires the regular pronominalization of the repeated NP. It further requires modification of the verb: the hitherto empty V position is filled with the function verb *have*. Since *have* is a V, it is capable of absorbing the tense, making the addition of *be* to M no longer necessary. The result of choosing the first L as subject results, through Subject– Preposition deletion, *have* insertion, Object–Preposition deletion, repeated NP pronominalization, and tense affixation, in:

The box has many toys in it. '

Certainly it is true that

Many toys are in the box,
There are many toys in the box,
The box has many toys in it,

are related, with variations in focus, although why Fillmore refers to the first as 'normal' is difficult to understand as it would seem to be the least common.
Unfortunately, Fillmore does not deal with the related problem of

There is a lock on the box,
The box has a lock (on it − or to it),

but not

> A lock is on the box (unless the lock is a separate item).

It is noticeable that when an item is a part of a bigger item, the Prepositional Phrase – *on it, to it* is optional. The same applies to plants, so that we have

> There are red flowers on this tree,

which we can say even if the flowers are not there at the present time, and

> This tree has red flowers (on it),

where, again, the *on it* is optional and does not imply that the flowers are on the tree at the present time although it is more likely to imply this unless we add a specific temporal phrase such as:

> This tree has red flowers on it in summer.

The relationships of the flowers to the tree (or a roof to a house, a door to a room, etc.) are not, however, quite the same as those of body parts to a human being. We do not normally say

> Joe has a big nose on him,

although in Cockney English, one might say for the same thing

> Joe has a whacking great conk on him.

Usually this addition of *on him* is for humorous effect and is not a common feature in English. Certainly, we do not have

> Joan has blue eyes on her (or in her),
> Fred has fair hair on him (unless it is someone else's hair).

Also we do not have clauses of the type

> There is a big nose on Joe,
> There are blue eyes on (or in) Joan,
> There is fair hair on Fred.

It is only when there is what is hoped to be a temporary addition to a body part that we have such constructions as

> Your nose has a wart on it,
> There is a boil on your neck.

The problem of Alienable and Inalienable Possession by animate beings will be discussed in the following chapters but the problem of fixed and moveable location as exemplified by the box having a lock as against the box having toys in it must be considered now.

If it be true that the difference between keeping a car in the garage and washing a car in the garage (as discussed under 3.1) is a matter of inner Locative as against outer Locative, then perhaps we may say that the box is an inner Locative in relation to the toys.

If we *put, keep* or *leave* many toys in the box, then it is true that

> The box has many toys in it,
> There are many toys in the box,
> Many toys are in the box.

However, it would hardly seem that the relationship of the handles to the box is one of outer Location or of far outer Location. Perhaps it is rather in the GM of *the toys* as against *the handles.* At the end of ch. 1, it was suggested that probably an Objective Case (or GM) was insufficient. We shall return to this problem in ch. 5 but it may be mentioned briefly here that instead of an Objective Case, there is need for two GMs: Affective and Neutral. These may be exemplified in the respective Objects of

> Joe cut the picture,
> Joe inspected the picture,

where in the first example, Joe *does* something to the picture whereas in the second he does not.

Although in the matter of the toys being in the box we are concerned with a static matter as against a dynamic one if they are *put* in the box, the GM relationships of the toys and the box seem to be the same. If

> Joe put the toys in the box,

is an example of toys having the GM of Affective, then it would seem that this is so if the toys are in the box.

On the other hand, we are not concerned with a static—dynamic relationship between things and their integral parts. Although man-made objects have had parts put together in many cases or parts put on to them, we generally think of a reasonably permanent relationship, like that of the box to its handles. In the case of a tree and its branches or flowers there is no connection with manufacture at all, and although the flowers may not be permanently on the tree they are on it seasonally. We might therefore consider that the handle of the box, or the flower on the tree has the GM Neutral. We might notice in passing that although we can have at Phrase Level

> The handles of the box,
> The roof of the house,
> The flowers of the tree,

we do not, of course, have

> The toys of the box,

but

> The toys in the box.

This again seems to suggest a more transitory relationship. It is, of course, possible to have such clauses as

> The roof is on that house,

when we wish to express the fact that there was no roof before but that it has recently been put on. This would be an Affective—Locative relationship like that of the toys in the box.

3.4. Physical contact with a body part

We must defer a fuller discussion of the Possession of body parts until we have discussed Alienable and Inalienable Possession. However, it is obvious that the relationship of *John* to *nose* is quite different from that of *John* to *his car*.

However, it is noticeable that although we can say

> Joe hit Bill's jaw,

or more commonly

> Joe hit Bill on the jaw,

we do not say

> Joe hit the box on its handle,

although we do say

> Joe hit the handle of the box.

Actually there are some instances where we do have clauses of the type

> X verb Y on/in part of Y,

especially when that Location is modified. Thus

> Joe hit the target right in the bullseye,
> Joe hit the nail (square) on the head,

but these seem to be limited, probably to when that 'part of Y' is referred to by the name of a body part. Even then

> Joe kicked the table in the leg,

sounds strange.

Fillmore suggests that 'sentences' like

> Mary pinched John on the nose

are derivable from deep structures of the type (Fillmore 1968a:68):

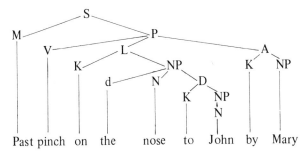

where

> on the nose to John

is dominated by L (Locative) and

> to John

is dominated by D (Dative).

It is difficult to know why Fillmore considers that *pinch, hit, strike,* etc., imply Locative, except for his statement (Fillmore 1968b:387) that 'there are languages which use a Locative case ending for nouns that go with verbs of hitting'.

Certainly, in a case like

> Joe hit Bill at the hotel,

the phrase

> at the hotel,

would, in our terms, be the filler of an outer Locative and would be an answer to

> Where did Joe hit Bill?

However, the response

> Joe hit Bill,

would not be what one would expect to

> Where did Joe hit?

but rather to

> Who(m) did Joe hit?

It is, of course, true that the question

> Where did Joe hit Bill?

might elicit the response

(Joe hit Bill) on the nose.

On the other hand, the question

Who(m) did you hit?

might elicit the response

Bill ... on the nose.

This suggests that we could take *Bill on the nose* as constituting one phrase. We can hardly consider that *on the nose* may be considered as an example of any of our previously discussed Clause Level Locatives. After all, Bill is not located *on* the nose in the same way that he would be located somewhere if we

put Bill into gaol,
washed Bill in the bathroom,
knew Bill in England.

In fact, *the nose* is actually located on Bill.
  Certainly, it is true that

Joe hit Bill's nose,
Joe hit Bill in/on the nose,

are related, although they are perhaps not quite as close as Fillmore would seem to suggest. The most feasible solution, within a tagmemic framework, might be to say that

Bill on the nose,

is a phrase of a type which may be a filler of a particular Grammatical Form– Meaning relationship. The Head of this phrase is filled by the Inalienable Possessor, in this instance Bill, and the optional Location tagmeme is filled by the Locative phrase which, because the Head is an Inalienable Possessor, refers to a body part of that Inalienable Possessor.
  On the other hand, in

Joe hit Bill's nose,

the *nose* is the Head and *Bill's* is the filler of a Subjunct representing the Inalienable Possessor.

In the case of Passive Clauses, there would be discontinuity as in

Bill was hit in/on the nose by Joe.

We shall return to the matter of Inalienable Possession when discussing further what Fillmore refers to as the Dative Case.

4. FURTHER GRAMMATICAL MEANINGS

4.0. Discussion of further Grammatical Meanings

It is obvious that further GMs need to be added to the list in ch. 2. We have suggested in chs. 2 and 3 that Objective may need to be subdivided into two distinct GMs and Fillmore has himself suggested (Fillmore 1968a:26 (fn. 34); 31) what might be called the Benefactive Case (B).

In this chapter I shall investigate Benefactive and the subdivision of Objective and suggest some further GMs which may be needed.

4.1. Benefactive

We could say that Benefactive is the GM concerned with the perceived beneficiary of an action or state. By beneficiary is meant the animate being (or human institution like *school, nation,* etc.) which is perceived as intended to benefit.

Benefactive is often indicated in English by a Prepositional Phrase commencing with *for* but this is not in itself necessarily indicative of Benefactive as in examples like

> I am going out for food,

the phrase

> for food

would be Purposive rather than Benefactive.

However, the Prepositional Phrase in:

> Joe is building a house *for Fred,*

would be Benefactive as Joe builds the house for Fred's benefet.
    Related to this example is:

> Joe is building *Fred* a house,

where Benefactive occurs without a Preposition. Again, Benefactive may occur
as Subject as in:

> *Fred* was built a house by Joe.

Thus, with *build* (and various other verbs like: *make, cook, bake*) Benefactive
may occur as Subject, Object or as a Prepositional Phrase.
    The problem remains whether Benefactive may occur with other verbs with
which the Prepositional Phrase would not commence with *for*. Fillmore seems
to suggest that verbs like *give* imply what he calls the Dative case. In fact (Fillmore 1968a:27) he suggests that *give* could be inserted into the frame
___O+D+A. Later (Fillmore 1968a:30) he suggests the same case frame for
show. Certainly, both of these verbs occur in overtly similar clauses:

> George gave/showed Mary the book,
> Georege gave/showed the book to Mary,
> Mary was given/shown the book by George,
> The book was given/shown to Mary by George.

However, related to the above is the clause

> George's gift to Mary was a book,

but we do not have anything like

> *George's showing to Mary was a book.

Furthermore, just as Mary would become the Alienable Possessor of a house
if George built her a house, so she may become the Alienable Possessor of the
book if George gives her a book.
    It would therefore seem that if the verb implies the Factitive GM as with
build or may have the Factitive GM as with *cook* (Factitive if one cooks, for
example, a meal) then the Prepositional Phrase with the GM Benefactive would
commence with *for*. If, on the other hand, the verb does not imply the GM
Factitive but may imply a change of ownership as with *give, donate,* then the

Prepositional Phrase with the GM Benefactive will commence with *to.*

It will be shown later that *give* is a verb which may imply various configurations of GM. We have been concerned so far with an Agent, in this case
George, handing a physical object to a person. However, a physical object may
be given without any actual handing from one person to another as in:

George gave his daughter a block of land.

Again, in English, giving includes the giving of *advice,* opinions, etc. That this
kind of giving is more akin to showing may be seen by comparing

Mary's gift from George was a book,
His daughter's gift from George was a block of land,

with

(?) Fred's gift from George was some advice.

In fact, we would hardly say

George's gift to Fred was some advice,

although this is closer to the acceptable

George's gift to Fred was advice based on his long
experience in the matter.

I would also claim that the GM Benefactive is implied by verbs which occur
in Agentless clauses. Thus, the possession of Alienable Possessions seems to
imply Benefactive. Thus in:

Fred has a car,

Fred would be a Subject with the GM Benefactive. Also at Phrase Level

Fred's car

would have *Fred's* as a Subjunct [1] with the GM Benefactive.

[1] At Phrase Level, a Subjunct tagmeme often stands in a qualifying relationship to
the Head tagmeme, e.g., 'popular' in 'this popular resort'.

4.1.1. *Inner and outer Benefactives*

Just as there are inner, outer and far outer Locatives, there appear to be inner, outer and far outer Benefactives.

The discussion so far has been concerned only with inner Benefactives where the animate being (or human institution) benefitting *is* or *becomes* the Alienable Possessor of something. However, there appears to be an outer Benefactive in such examples as

> I'll walk the dog for you,
> I'll clean the house for you.

The person represented by *you* in each case does not become the Alienable Possessor of the *dog* or *house.* It is true that the person *may* own the dog or house but this is not implied and we would need to add *your* in each case to make this clear. However, the person represented by *you* is meant to be the beneficiary of the action in each case. Furthermore, we always have the option of indicating that the beneficiary *is* the Alienable Possessor.

There is the problem of such examples as:

> I'll wash your face for you,

where the action to be performed concerns an Inalienable Possession of the beneficiary. We do not, in present-day English, have such clauses as

> I'll wash you your face.

Therefore it seems that *for you* must be considered here as an example of an outer Benefactive. The verb *wash* implies an Agent and as the Agent does not perform an action which leads to the beneficiary becoming the Alienable Possessor, then it may take an outer Benefactive.

Although far outer Locatives may co-occur with any verb, even with one like *resemble* in

> In that region, the houses resemble beehives,

this does not seem to be the case with far outer Benefactives. Thus, if

> For you, the houses resemble beehives,

means anything it is more in the nature of: 'In your opinion' or 'To your way of thinking' that the houses resemble beehives. There is certainly no benefit implied. In fact, *for you* could be combined with various clauses with all sorts of meanings as in:

> For me, she is the best student in the group,
> For me, that house is too big.

However, there are verbs which imply an Agent who performes some mental or physical process which neither leads to Alienable Possession by an animate being (or institution) nor in any way affects anything which *could* be owned by the beneficiary. Thus, we have examples like:

> For you, Jimmy is being good,
> For her, I'd walk a mile.

These far outer Benefactives may, like far outer Locatives, occur in clause initial or final position and are usually separated from the rest of the clause by commas in writing or be definite prosodic features including a perceived pause in speech.

4.2. A Grammatical Meaning Purposive

Such examples as

> Tom is going out for some milk,
> Jack dug a hole for water,

suggest that there is a GM Purposive. In both of these examples, the Purposive tagmeme is filled by a prepositional phrase commencing with *for*.

If we try to find Passive clauses related to these, we can see that there is no Passive (or pseudo-passive) clause related to the former nor a clause with *water* as Subject related to the latter. Thus we do not have

> *Some milk is being gone out for by Joe,
> *Water is being dug a hole for by Jack,

but only

> A hole was dug by Jack for water,

and even this seems rather clumsy.

A diagnostic test for Purposive is: 'For what purpose is something done?'

Thus we may ask

> For what purpose is Joe going out?
> For what purpose did Jack dig a hole?

and the answers would be

> for some milk,
> for water.

Apparently similar to the preceding examples are such ones as

> Tom looked for a book,
> Mary is asking for your article,

but there are several differences. Firstly it may be noticed that the verb + preposition in *look for* and *ask for* are 'kept together' by prosodic features whereas in 'go out ... for' and 'dig a hole ... for' they are not. Secondly, we may substitute one lexical item for *look for,* namely *seek* or for *ask for,* namely *demand* or *request.* This is not possible with *go out for* or *dig for.* Thirdly, we would hardly ask

> For what purpose did Tom look?
> For what purpose is Mary asking?

but rather

> What did Tom look for?
> What is Mary asking for?

Fourthly, there are Passive clauses with *ask for* and *look for,* related to our examples

> A book is being looked for by Tom,
> Your article is being asked for by Mary.

Both of these seem rather inelegant but Passive clauses with *look for* and *ask for* of a more acceptable kind do occur with other lexical items

> Your letter will be looked for by all the staff,
> This book was constantly asked for (by a great many students).

However, there is the problem that with *ask (for)* we do also have such examples as

> Mary asked Tom for a book,
> Tom was asked for a book by Mary.

It might be argued that the discontinuity of the first of these would suggest that we cannot consider *ask for* as constituting a Predicate filler. However, there are the many examples of what are sometimes considered as verb + particle where there may be discontinuity as with:

> Claude wrote up his report / Claude wrote his report up,
> Jill sent off a letter / Jill sent a letter off.

Interestingly, if we substitute *request* or *demand* for *ask,* we have:

> Mary requested/demanded a book of/from Tom,
> A book was requested/demanded of/from Tom (by Mary).

Thus with *ask for* it is the person asked who may appear as subject but with *request* and *demand* it is the thing requested or demanded which may appear as subject. This would seem to show that these verbs are so idiosyncratic in this respect that to specify general transformations in this case is impossible. What is necessary is that we set up co-occurrence relationships for each verb. We may then find that two or more verbs always occur in exactly the same relationships to other elements in the clause but we can see that *ask for* and *request* do not have exactly the same co-occurrence relationships although it is possible that *request* and *demand* do.

4.3. A possible Grammatical Meaning Directional

Fillmore (1968a:25) suggests that 'locational and directional elements do not contrast but are superficial differences determined either by the constituent structure or by the character of the associated verb'. It would seem that Directional is a type of inner Locative. Some verbs like *put* co-occur with prepositions like *in, under, on,* which seem to be Locative but they also co-occur with *into, on to,* which seem to be Directional. Other verbs like *send, post,* do not co-occur with Locative type prepositions but only Directional type prepositions like *to.* In this we have been concerned only with inner Locatives — obviously one can send a letter *at the Post Office* (outer Locative).

4.4. Other Grammatical Meanings

Fillmore considers that *rob* and *steal* (Fillmore 1968b:388) imply his Dative Case. Others might consider that these verbs and also *lose* would imply and that *take* would co-occur with a Deprivative Case or GM. However, if we take Fillmore's definition of Dative 'the case of the animate being (and add 'or human institution') affected by the state or action identified by the verb' then the person or human institution who is robbed, has something stolen from him or taken from him or who loses something would fit into this category.

4.5. Comitative

Again Fillmore (1968a:81) has suggested a Comitative Case and refers to Jespersen's noticing 'the parallels between *with* (a preposition which has a comitative function) and the conjunctor *and*, as in such pairs of sentences as 185 and 186 (1924, p.90).

185   He and his wife are coming.
186   He is coming with his wife.'

However, he concludes by stating: 'It is quite unlikely that the numerous problems associated with NP conjunction can be appreciably simplified through this approach, but that there is some connection between conjunction and comitative uses of NP's cannot be doubted. Lakoff and Peters (1966) have recently presented very persuasive arguments that the 'direction' of the relationship is the opposite of what I have suggested; that, in other words, comitative phrases are derived from NP conjunction rather than the other way around.'

Fillmore does not make it clear whether he would have reserved Comitative for example such as the one he quotes from Jespersen or whether he would also include

Harry is coming with his ukelele,
Mary is coming with her baby,
Jack is coming with his dog.

In the first of these examples, *Harry* is certainly the only Agent and it is more likely that we would interpret *Mary* and *Jack* as the only Agents in the other examples, too. Although we may say

Harry and his ukelele are coming,
Mary and her baby are coming
Jack and his dog are coming,

we still assume that only *Harry*, *Mary* and *Jack* are the Agents. On the other hand

> Harry is building a house with Fred,
> Harry and Fred are building a house,

imply that both *Harry* and *Fred* are Agents. Thus, *with Fred* would be a Clause Level tagmeme with the GMs Comitative and Agentive. *Fred* in the second example would also be both Agentive and Comitative. However, in

> Harry and Fred are building houses,

Fred would be Comitative only if this were related to

> Harry is building houses with Fred,

and not if they were not associated in a building project.

We are quite aware of the problem of such examples as:

> Harry is building with Bloggs and Co.,

where *Harry* is employed by *Bloggs and Co.* Bloggs and Co. are probably here beneficiaries of Harry's building work and so it might be considered that they are at once Benefactive and Comitative. In our previous examples it would seem that the speaker/writer and the listener/reader would consider the first mentioned as in some way either more important or the initiator of the action as in

> Smith entered with an important guest.

However, a great deal depends on the reader/listener's knowledge of the whole situation. Interestingly in Kukata, one may have:

> *patu ulat-^{y}ara janu*   'The man came with the child',
> *patu papat-^{y}ara janu* 'The man came with the dog'.

but hardly the reverse. In Kukata and also in Pitjantjatjara, the affix *-t-^{y}ara* always has a Comitative meaning. In fact the name of the latter, in full *waŋka pit-^{y}aŋt-^{y}at-^{y}ara*, the speech with (or having) *pit-^{y}ant-^{y}a* (a form of the verb 'to come') illustrates this too.

5. OBJECTIVE AND DATIVE

5.0.

It was suggested in sections 2.3.2 and 3.3 that what Fillmore refers to as the Objective Case seems to be too wide. In this chapter, I shall discuss the need for two Grammatical Meanings instead of the one Objective and also what Fillmore refers to as the Dative Case.

5.1. Affiziertes and effiziertes Objekt

Fillmore (1968a:4) illustrates the distinction between Affectum and Effectum or, in German, affiziertes Objekt and effiziertes Objekt with the examples

(1)   John ruined the table,
(2)   John built the table.

He goes on to show 'that one might relate sentence 1, but not sentence 2, to the question given in 3.

(3)   What did John do to the table?',

and he suggests that 'while sentence 1 has sentence 4 as a paraphrase, sentence 5 is not a paraphrase of sentence 2.

(4)   What John did to the table was ruin it,
(5)   What John did to the table was build it.

As Fillmore (1968b:387) seems to suggest that *break* implies his Objective Case for what gets broken we must assume that he would consider that *ruin* similarly imples the Objective. However, these two verbs, *break* and *ruin* would also imply an Agent who does the breaking or ruining. Therefore we should be able to compare these two verbs with others that Fillmore suggests as implying Agentive and Objective, or, at least may occur with Agentive and Objective. These include: *open, cook, listen, look, learn, show,* this last also implying 'Dative'. Let us try Fillmore's question 3 with these and also his paraphrase as illustrated in (4) above:

What did John do to the door?
What John did to the door was open it.

What did John do to the steak?
What John did to the steak was cook it.

What did John do to the music?
What John did to the music was listen to it. **

What did John do to the painting?
What John did to the painting was look at it. **

What did John do to the lesson?
What John did to the lesson was learn it. **

What did John do to the book?
What John did to the book was show it to Ann.

What did John do to the university?
What John did to the University was show it to Ann. **

All of the examples marked ** seem very stange. I would therefore propose that the verbs: *open* and *cook* may be said to imply the GM of Affective (although as will be illustrated later, *cook* may imply in certain circumstances Factitive instead of Affective). On the other hand the verbs: *listen, look, learn* would imply the GM Neutral where nothing is *done* to anything at all. *See* and *know,* verbs which according to Fillmore imply Dative and Objective should be considered as implying the GM Neutral.

If we are to use Fillmore's question as a discovery procedure for Affective, then it would seem that *show* may imply the Affective GM, as illustrated in the showing of a *book* but it may alternatively imply Neutral as illustrated in the showing of the university. The reason would seem to be that we *may,* although not necessarily so, actually hand a book to someone when we show it but quite obviously we do not do so with the university, Melbourne or such other not readily moveable objects.

I would consider, therefore, that verbs like: *hit, bash, destroy, cut, damage* may co-occur with the GM Affective while verbs like: *fear, like, indicate, smell* (in regard to what is smelt), *notice* imply the GM Neutral. Verbs like *show, give, donate* may co-occur with the GMs Affective or Neutral, according to whether or not the Agent *does* something to whatever is shown, given or accepted. Thus we may have

> What John did to the book was show it to Ann,
> What John did to the book was give it to Ann,
> What John did to the book was donate it to Ann.

But we can hardly substitute *block of land* for *book.*

5.2. Dative — Participative

It has been suggested already in ch. 4 that *give* may imply the GM Benefactive. That is that if any physical item is given to any animate being or human institution with the intention of its becoming the alienable possession of that animate being or human institution then we can consider the animate being or human institution to whom it is given as having the GM Benefactive.

It has already been suggested in chs. 3 and 4 that we need to discriminate between Alienable and Inalienable Possession and that Alienable Possession involves the GM Benefactive. We must consider further the matter of Inalienable Possession.

Fillmore's definition, as we have seen, of his Dative Case is 'the case of the animate being affected by the state or action identified by the verb'. It was suggested in section 2.3.2 that this be changed by inserting 'usually or typically' before animate. Alternatively, we could modify 'animate being' to 'animate being or human institution'.

Fillmore's choice of the term Dative seems unfortunate as it cannot help but have connotations of Indirect Object or the German and Latin Dative Cases. Therefore, I would propose another name. First, however, it will be necessary to redefine our definition of this particular GM. To illustrate this, we may consider the following examples, where the italicized words all examplify this GM

> *Fred* likes hamburgers,
> George irritated *Claude,*
> Mary pointed out the Cultural Centre *to Doris,*
> Bloggs murdered *a warder,*
> *Jack* saw the film,
> *Henry* knows the answer.

It will be noticed that whenever this GM occurs as Subject, we do not usually have a corresponding Imperative clause. Thus, we do not have

> Like hamburgers!
> Know the answer!

nor, to take some other examples

> Fear that dog!
> Hate that man!
> Suspect Bloggs!

However, we do say

> See that film! It's really worth seeing,

but hardly:

> See spots before your eyes!

Thus, when a person is told to *see* something, we could consider this as almost synonymous with *look at* and consider the person who is told to see as Agentive.

What is common to all our examples above is that the person concerned is emotionally (as with *irritate*), mentally (as with *know*), or sensually (as with *Doris*) involved in the state or action indicated by the verb *without being an Agent*. Whatever a person's religious beliefs, he will probably feel that a person who is murdered is mentally or sensually involved in the action. We would also consider that *die* implies the same GM.

Inalienable possession also implies that one is sensually involved. One can feel a pain in one's big toe, one can be hurt in the leg. However, *hair* is on a borderline between being alienably and inalienably possessed. We are more likely to say:

> Lucy is the owner of a beautiful head of red hair,

than

> Lucy is the owner of beautiful red cheeks.

Generally, we may *have* alienable or inalienable possessions but we *own* or *possess* alienable possessions.

Some languages, like Pitjantjatjara clearly indicate alienable and inalienable possessions as with:

> watiku kulạta   'the man's spear',
> wati t·ʸina   'the man's foot',

and interestingly family relationships are marked as alienable:

> watiku mama   'the man's father'.

However, in English, although we may *own* or *possess* a spear, we do not *own* or *possess* a father any more than we do a foot. Thus it would seem that the Alienable–Inalienable distinction, which is probably indicated somehow in every language, encompasses different groups of possessions in various languages.

Thus, to cover what we wish to indicate by this particular GM, I suggest the name Participative and give the following definition: Participative – the GM of the tagmeme indicating the animate being or human institution, not itself an Agent which is emotionally, mentally or sensually involved in the state or action indicated by the verb.

6. GRAMMATICAL FORM AND GRAMMATICAL MEANING

6.0. Language particulars and language universals

For every language it is necessary to consider Grammatical Form, the overt occurrences and relationships of what have traditionally been called: Subjects, Objects, Complements, Adjuncts and so on and Grammatical Meaning, what we have considered as Agentive, Benefactive and so on and the interrelationships of these. Thus it is necessary to consider what GMs co-occur with particular verbs, which of these *must* occur, which are implied without any overt occurrence and so on.

Terms like Subject and Object are language particular and different criteria are needed for determining what is a Subject in, for example, English and Pitjantjatjara.

However, GMs would seem to be language universal. Thus in all languages Agents, Benefactives and Locatives can be found. Obviously, in a particular language, Agentives may always appear as Subject, in another Factitives may always appear before Benefactives and so on. Again, Locatives and Instrumentals may always be similarly affixed but may occur in different positions in the clause.

My previous remarks about Subject and Object should not be taken as implying that these terms are not useful. It is obviously useful to be able to say that a Subject typically occurs in clause initial position in a particular language or that verbs 'agree' with the Subject. However, what appears to be unnecessary is an attempt to find any universal criteria for Subject.

A quotation from Fillmore (1968b:382) should make clear what is meant by stating that GMs would seem to be language universal: 'I believe that human languages are constrained in such a way that the relations between arguments and predicates fall into a small number of types. In particular, I believe that these role types can be identified with certain quite elementary judgments about the things that go on around us: judgments about who does something, who experiences something, who benefits from something, where something happens, what it is that changes, what it is that moves, where it starts out, and where it ends up. Since judgments like these are very much like the kinds of things grammarians have associated for centuries with the uses of grammatical 'cases', I have been referring to these roles as case relationships, or simply, cases.'

6.1. Grammatical Form

As was suggested above, criteria for determining Grammatical Form, that is Subject, Object and so on are language particular. We must now consider what criteria are needed for determining these in English.

6.1.1. *Subject* (S)

The Subject in English is that noun or noun substitute with which the verb agrees (if the verb shows agreement) [1] in number and person (to the extent that such agreement is shown in English). Thus a Subject tagmeme may be filled by a noun, pronoun, noun phrase or clause. Thus we may have, as examples of fillers of the Subject tagmeme:

> Fred worries me,
> That man worries me,
> He worries me,
> That he is coming tomorrow worries me.

Because of our criterion that in English, the Subject agrees with the verb, we shall, of necessity, have to consider that the Subject in such clauses as:

> There is a book on my shelf,
> There are books on my shelf,

are respectively *a book* and *books.*

Becker (1967:93) suggests that 'for the present it seems most reasonable to consider *there* a dummy Subject for S_{prop} and S_{loc}, and add a rule at word level that in the context # there ____, BE is governed by the following tagmeme. This is an unsatisfying, ad hoc rule. It works but it gives us no great insight into the working of *there* as a dummy subject.'

---

[1] This condition is to cover auxiliaries such as: will, can, may. However, it is usually possible to replace auxiliary + verb, e.g., *can work* by *work(s)*.

Becker illustrates the problem of *there* with the following set of sentences:

(a)   In the room are four windows,
(b)   *Four windows are in the room,
(c)   There are four windows in the room.

He then adds a tag question to each to obtain

(a′)   In the room are four windows, aren't there?
(b′)   *Four windows are in the room, aren't they?
(c′)   There are four windows in the room, aren't there?

and asks why (b) and (b′) do not occur. Let us substitute *men* for windows and examine the examples again

(d)   In the room are four men,
(e)   Four men are in the room,
(f)   There are four men in the room,

and, adding the tag question

(d′)   In the room are four men, aren't there?
(e′)   Four men are in the room, aren't there/they?
(f′)   There are four men in the room, aren't there?

We could say that the *men* are fillers of a Subject agentive tagmeme, whereas the windows fill a Subject neutral tagmeme as discussed in section 3.3. Let us again substitute another item into the same frame, namely *parcels*

(g)   In the room are four parcels,
(h)   Four parcels are in the room,
(i)   There are four parcels in the room,

and, adding the tag question

(g′)   In the room are four parcels, aren't there?
(h′)   Four parcels are in the room, aren't there?
(i′)   There are four parcels in the room, aren't there?

This, of course, is akin to the toys in the box discussed in section 3.3 and we could say that as the parcels are not a 'permanent' feature of the room, they may be considered as fillers of a $Subject_{affective}$ tagmeme.

We can see that if the clause contains a $Subject_{neutral}$ and an $Adjunct_{locative}$, then with *be,* we do not have clauses of the type

$$+ Subject_{neutral} + BE + Adjunct_{locative} ,$$

although if the verb is not *be* we do have clauses of this type:

> An old red gum stands over towards Blackburn Road.

Thus, *there* is a part of the Predicate and it is obligatorily preposed to *be* when *be* co-occurs with $Subject_{neutral}$ alone or with $Subject_{neutral}$ + Adjunct. It may optionally co-occur with *be* when the Subject is Agentive or Affective and an $Adjunct_{locative}$ also occurs in the clause. It may also be preposed to verbs like *lie, stand, exist* when the Subject is neutral and an $Adjunct_{locative}$ also occurs in the clause.

These rules would also cover Becker's (1967:93) further examples

> (8)   There is no doubt that John is frightened,
> (8′)   There are some doubts that John is frightened, aren't there?
>   *Some doubts are that John is frightened.

So

> No doubt/some doubts that John is frightened,

can be considered as fillers of a $Subject_{neutral}$ tagmeme and therefore the asterisked form would not occur. Nor would

> *Some doubts that John is frightened are,
> *No doubt that John is frightened is,
> *No doubt that John is frighted is at this meeting.

However,

> There is no doubt at this meeting that John is frightened,
> At this meeting there is no doubt that John is frightened,
> There is no doubt that John is frightened at this meeting,

are all acceptable. *At this meeting* would be an outer Locative. (It is realized that the third example is multiply ambiguous which is why this would be less likely than the other two. John could be frightened *of* the meeting and again he could be frightened when at the meeting in which cases *at the meeting* would not be a filler of a tagmeme in the main clause.)

We are still left with the problem of *it* which Becker (1967:91) raises before his discussion of *there*. I have already discussed in section 3.2 the problem of

> Chicago is windy,
> It is windy in Chicago,

where it was suggested that *it* is a pro form for 'atmosphere'. The same would hold for Becker's example

(25)   It is warmer on the south side.

However, there is the problem of

(6)   That John is frightened never occurred to me,
(7)   It never occurred to me that John is frightened.

We would agree with Becker that *it* may replace a category word like *idea* but we would not agree that a category word such as *idea* and a that-clause *may not* co-occur. In many varieties of English, his example

> It amuses me, the idea that John is frightened,

is perfectly acceptable, as are

> It amuses me, the belief that Jim holds,
> They irritate me, the views that Smith propounds.

Thus it would seem that *it* and *they* occur in pre-verb position whenever a Subject$_{neutral}$ is filled by a clause and is postponed. In fact, *it, they, he* and *she* may thus occur in pre-verb position in connection with other types of subjects, thus:

> It killed the cat, that nasty fierce dog (Subject$_{agentive}$),
> She fears the consequences, that stupid looking girl
> with blue eyes and a long nose (Subject$_{participative}$),
> It's been damaged, that interesting old antique chair
> I was telling you about (Subject$_{affective}$),

It's built at last, the long awaited Sydney Opera House
(Subject $_{factitive}$).

It seems that, in general, the preposing of *it, they, he, she* occurs when the Subject is long and when the speaker/writer wishes to introduce the verb without too long a delay. Thus I agree with Becker (1967:92) that 'the subject has moved out of focus'. However, as has been shown, I cannot agree with him that 'a tagmeme cannot be replaced anaphorically by both a pronoun *and* a category word at once, unless some such device as parenthesis is used:

That John is frightened never occurred to me,
It (the idea) never entered my mind,'

unless 'at once' means *consecutively* with the pronoun preceding. We can have

It never entered my mind, the idea,
The idea, it never entered my mind,

although these would seem less likely than where *it* stands for a tagmeme with more fillers as in

It never entered my mind, such a stupid, half-baked idea,
Such a stupid, half-baked idea, it never entered my mind.

From this discussion it is clear that there is no need to revise the definition of the Subject in English except to state that a Subject may be postponed to a post-verb position when *there* occurs as a part of the predicate or when *it, they, he, she* occur as dummy Subjects. In the latter case, there is agreement in number (and if singular and human — in gender) with the postponed referent.

6.1.2. *Object* (O)

If the Subject in English is 'that noun or noun substitute with which the verb agrees' then it can be said that the Object in English is that noun or noun substitute in a clause which is not the Subject but which would occur as Subject in the related Passive Clause. Thus if by definition, *Jim* is the Subject of

Jim ate the biscuits,

and *the biscuits* are the Subject of

> The biscuits were eaten by Joe,

then *the biscuits* must be the Object of the first clause. This discussion may appear trite. We all 'know' what an Object is in English. However, a formal definition may be useful.

Because we are considering Grammatical Meaning as well as Grammatical Form, there is no need for such terms as Direct Object and Indirect Object. Thus, in

> Tom gave Mary a book,

Mary is a filler of $Object_{participative}$ or $Object_{benefactive}$ and *a book* is a filler of $Object_{affective}$ (or, in some cases, $Object_{neutral}$). Again, in

> Tom gave a book to Mary,

a book is a filler of $Object_{affective}$ (or $Object_{neutral}$) but *to Mary* is not an Object because it is *not* simply a noun or noun substitute.

Again, by definition, there are no Objects in

> Jenny resembles her sister,
> Dick is a plumber,

because there are no related Passive Clauses in which *her sister* and *a plumber* occur as Subjects.

6.1.3. *Adjunct* (A)

Following Becker, I use the term Adjunct for a Clause Level prepositional phrase or prepositional phrase substitute. Thus *by George* is an $Adjunct_{agentive}$ in:

> Tom was stopped by George,

and *there* is an example of an $Adjunct_{locative}$ in:

> Tom put the car there.

However, this term must be further defined as a prepositional phrase could occur as filler of a Subject function as in:

> *Over the wall* is out.

It could hardly be claimed that *out* is the Subject and *over the wall* the Adjunct. Although we can also say

> Out is over the wall,

over the wall is not actually the location of *out*. We are saying that in this particular game, *over the wall* means that the player is out just as in some other game we could say that:

> The lowest score is out.

We can also see that if we conjoin two similar Subjects, we have verb agreement as in

> *Over the wall* and *over the hedge* are out.

   Therefore we need to define Adjunct as a prepositional phrase or prepositional phrase substitute not being the filler of a Subject or Object function. In addition, it may not be substituted by a noun or noun substitute without a preceding preposition. Thus, with

> *Over the wall* is out,

we could substitute

> *That area/place* is out,

but with

> Joe walked *to Melbourne,*

we cannot substitute *Melbourne* or any other noun or noun substitute for *to Melbourne.* Thus

> Joe walked Melbourne,

would only be grammatical if *Melbourne* were, for example, the name of a dog or horse.

6.1.4. *Complement* (C)

Complement can be defined as a noun or noun substitute which is not the Subject or Object of a clause. Thus, the verb does not agree with it as it does with the Subject and it would not occur as Subject in a related Passive Clause as is the case with the Object. Thus, in

> Joe resembles *Fred,*

Fred would be the Complement as we do not have a related clause

> Fred is resembled by Joe.

Also, in

> They elected Tom *president,*

we do not have a related clause with *president* as Subject and *they* and *Tom* appearing as Object or Adjunct as would be the case with

> They gave Tom a book,

where, if *book* occurs as Subject of a related Passive Clause, *Tom* and *them* occur as Adjuncts.[2]

6.1.5. *Predicate* (P)

The Predicate includes a verb which agrees with the Subject (if there is any agreement) and may be defined as any of:

(a) the verb phrase as in

> Claude *eats* pickles,
> Agatha *will be coming* tonight.

(b) the verb or verb phrase + particle as in

> Fred *bashed up* Jim,
> Fred *bashed* Jim *up.*

(c) the verb or verb phrase + preposition if the verb or verb phrase + preposition may occur consecutively in a passive clause. Thus

---

[2] In some dialects, *Tom* could occur as Object.

Bill *trod on* the peanut,
The peanut *was trodden on* by Bill.

However, *in* would not be within the Predicate Phrase in

Milly sat in the corner,

as there is not a passive clause of the type:

*The corner was sat in by Milly.

(d) *be, become, grow, turn* + Adjective. We can see that these may be considered as Predicate fillers because of the similarity between the pairs:

Mary is sulky,	Mary sulks,
The cheese became mature,	The cheese matured,
Tom has grown old,	Tom has aged,
Fred quickly turns angry,	Fred angers quickly.

Furthermore, we may conjoin predicates filled by verbs and those filled by *be, become, grow, turn* + adjective. Thus we may have:

Mary sulks and is moody,
The cheese matured and became tasty,
Tom has withered and grown old,
Fred quickly angers and turns nasty.

However, this is not possible with Predicate + Complement conjoined with Predicate. We do not have:

Mary sulks and is a neighbour,
The cheese matured and is a Camembert,
Tom has withered and become a butcher,
Fred turned angry and was a doctor.

6.2. Grammatical Meaning

The GMs (discussed in previous chapters) are given below together with certain discovery procedures particular to English.

6.2.1. *Affective* (aff)

The entity affected by the action or state.

(1) A tagmeme with the GM Affective need not be filled by noun phrase with a head representing an animate being or institution of animate being.

(2) Does not occur as GM in Complement tagmemes.

(3) Imperative test does not work. If occurring in Subject tagmemes, there is no related Imperative clause such that

$$+ S_{aff} + P : \text{non-imperative verb form ...}$$

is related to

$$+ P : \text{imperative verb form ...}$$

(4) If occurring in an Object tagmeme and the GM of the Subject tagmeme is Agentive, there is a relationship such that

$$+ S_{ag} + P + O_{aff}$$

is related to

$$\text{WHAT } S_{ag} \text{ DO to } O_{aff} \text{ is P it.}$$

Thus

Joe broke the vase,

is related to

What Joe did to the vase was break it.

This will be referred to as the WHAT DO test.

6.2.2. *Agentive* (ag)

Instigator of the action; typically animate (except in the case of natural forces or mechanical devices).

(1) If occurring in a Subject tagmeme, the Imperative test works:

$$+ S_{ag} + P : \text{non-imperative verb form ...}$$

is related to

$$+ P : \text{imperative verb form ...}$$

e.g.,

> Joe weeded the garden,
> Weed the garden!

(2) If this GM occurs in an Adjunct tagmeme, the filler will commence with *by* but this is not of itself a sufficient criterion, as Adjuncts commencing with *by* may have GM Instrumental or GM Participative.

(3) Does not occur in Object or Complement tagmemes.

(4) Co-occurs freely with Adjunct tagmemes filled by Manner Adverbials.

(5) May always co-occur with Predicates which may be filled by + BE + verb-ing, e.g.,

> *Jim is eating his lunch*

(but not

> *Jim is resembling Jack*).

6.2.3. *Benefactive*

Perceived beneficiary of action or state (i.e. the animate being or human institution which is perceived as intended to benefit.)

6.2.3.1. *Benefactive (inner)* (ben-i)

(1) If occurring in Adjunct tagmemes, will commence with *for* (not expandable as *for the purpose of* but *for the benefit of*) if co-occurring with Factitive, *to* if not co-occurring with Factitive but with Affective.

(2) If occurring in a Subject or Object tagmeme and the GMs Agentive and Affective/Factitive also occur in tagmemes of the same clause construction, the clause will be related to one where the GM ben-i occurs in an Adjunct tagmeme:

(a) $\quad + S_{ben-i} \; + P :$ verb passive $+ O_{aff \; or \; fact} \pm Ad_{ag}$

(b) $\quad + S_{ag} \quad + P :$ verb active $\; + O_{ben-i} + O_{aff \; or \; fact}$

are related to:

(c) $\quad + S_{ag} \; +P :$ verb active $+ O_{aff \; or \; fact} + Ad_{ben-i}$

examples (GM ben-i is italicized in each case):

(a)   *Mary* was bought a book by Fred,

(b)   Fred bought *Mary* a book,

are related to

(c)   Fred bought a book *for Mary.*

(3) If occurring in a Complement tagmeme, the filler will be a possessive noun phrase (e.g., *Jack's, that man's*) as in

This book is Jack's.

(4) A tagmeme with the GM ben-i must have as the noun phrase head of its filler a noun or pronoun representing an animate being or institution of animate beings, e.g.,

He built *his father-in-law* a tool shed.

(5) May not co-occur with outer Benefactives.

6.2.3.2. *Benefactive (outer)* (ben-o)
     (1) Occurs only in an Adjunct tagmeme whose filler commences with *for* (the benefit of).
     (2) A tagmeme with the GM ben-o must have as the noun phrase head of its filler a noun or pronoun representing an animate being or institution of animate beings, e.g.,

I'll prune the roses for you.

(3) The head of the noun phrase occurring in the Benefactive Adjunct does not *become* an alienable possessor through the action represented by the verb and *need* not be such a possessor.
     (4) May occur in tagmemes in clause initial or clause final position, e.g.,

For you, I'll prune the roses.

(5) May not co-occur with inner Benefactives.

6.2.3.3. *Benefactive (far-outer)* (ben-fo)
     (1) Occurs only in an Adjunct tagmeme whose filler commences with *for* (the benefit of), e.g.,

For her, Jack will run a mile and jump a stile.

(2) May occur in tagmemes in clause initial or clause final position.

(3) Must co-occur with the GM Agentive but not necessarily with any other.

(4) If co-occurring with the GM Affective or the GM Participative, the head of the noun phrase in the Benefactive tagmeme may not be the alienable or inalienable possessor of the item represented by the head of the filler of the Affective or Participative tagmeme.

(5) May co-occur with inner or outer Benefactives, e.g.,

> *For you,* I even wash Dad's car.

6.2.4. *Factitive* (fact)

The entity resulting from action or state.

(1) If occurring in an Adjunct tagmeme, the filler will commence with to/into, e.g.,

> She made the dough *into dumplings.*

(2) If occurring in a Subject tagmeme:

(a) The Predicate tagmeme will be filled by a passive verbal construction and an Adjunct tagmeme with the GM Agentive may occur:

> *Those slums* were built by Marmeduke.

or

(b) the verbal filler of the Predicate tagmeme will be in an active form and the GM Agentive may not occur:

> *The leaves* sprouted.

(3) If occurring in an Object tagmeme or in a Subject tagmeme as in (a) above, it may co-occur with the GM ben-i:

> Lulu cooked *a meal* for Algy.

(4) WHAT DO test will not produce a meaningful sentence.

6.2.5. *Instrumental* (inst)

Force or object causally involved in the action or state.

(1) May always co-occur with the GM Agentive (overtly manifested):

> Jo tickled Flo *with a blade of grass.*

(2) If occurring in an Object tagmeme, there must be a Subject tagmeme with the GM Agentive, e.g.,

> He used *a tooth pick.*

(3) If occurring in Adjunct tagmemes, the filler will commence with (a) *with* if co-occurring with the GM Agentive, or (b) *with* or *by* if this is not the case.

(4) Not necessarily filled by a noun phrase with head representing an animate being or institution.

6.2.6. *Locative*
Location or spatial orientation of the state or action.

6.2.6.1. *Locative (inner)* (loc-i)
(1) If it occurs in an Adjunct tagmeme, the filler is a locational adverb such as *here, there,* or a locational proposition such as *in, on, under* or a directional preposition such as *into, to,* followed by the noun phrase; e.g.,

> Fred sat *there.*

(2) Is an obligatory GM with some verbs, e.g.,

> Mary put the antimacassar onto the armchair.

(3) If an Agent occurs, it is not located in the location represented by the filler of the tagmeme with the GM of inner Locative, e.g.,

> Joe puts his car *into the garage.*

(Joe is *not* originally in the garage.)
(4) Does not occur in Complement tagmemes.
(5) Does not co-occur with the GM outer Locative in the same clause construction.

6.2.6.2. *Locative (outer)* (loc-o)
(1) Does not occur in Complement tagmemes.
(2) Does not co-occur with inner Locative in the same clause construction.
(3) If occurring in an Adjunct tagmeme, the filler commences with a preposition representing location and not direction.
(4) The tagmeme with the GM outer Locative usually indicates the location

of the being or institution which is the head [3] of the filler construction of tag-memes with GM Agentive or GM Instrumental, e.g.,

Marty works *in a chewing-gum factory*,

(i.e., Marty *is* in the factory).
  (5) Must co-occur with the GMs Agentive or Participative.

6.2.6.3. *Locative (far-outer)* (loc-fo)
  (1) Always occurs in Adjunct tagmemes, e.g.,

In Collingwood, many people keep their cars in the street.

  (2) May co-occur with GM inner Locative or GM outer Locative.
  (3) Occurs freely in tagmemes in clause initial or final position.
  (4) Co-occurs with any verb.
  (5) Need not co-occur with the GMs Agentive, Instrumental or Participative.

6.2.7. *Neutral* (neut)
  An entity which is in no way affected by the action or state.
  (1) WHAT DO test does not work.
  (2) Imperative test does not work.
  (3) A tagmeme with the GM Neutral may co-occur in the same clause con-struction with another tagmeme with the GM Neutral:

That tree is *a Eucalyptus camaldulensis.*

6.2.8. *Participative* (part)
  Animate being or human institution (not itself an agent) which is emotion-ally, mentally or sensually involved in the state or action.
  (1) May occur in Subject, Object or Adjunct tagmemes.
  (2) Imperative test does not work, e.g.,

*Like that apple!

  (3) WHAT DO test does not freely work, e.g.,

---

[3] Strictly speaking, it would be the filler of the head tagmeme in the phrase construc-tion which serves as filler to the clause level tagmemes with the above mentioned GMs.

> Joe liked his grandmother,
> *What Joe did to his grandmother was like her.

(4) If occurring in Adjunct tagmemes, the filler will often commence with *by* or *to*.

> He was liked *by all his staff*,
> Cynthia whispered *to Claude*.

(5) Occurs only in tagmemes having as fillers noun phrases where the head tagmeme is filled by a noun or pronoun representing an animate being or an institution.

6.2.9. *Purposive* (purp)
Purpose of action or state
(1) Occurs only in Adjunct tagmemes, e.g.,

> This vessel is used for cooking.

(2) Must co-occur with the GM Agentive, even if not overtly manifested.
(3) In Adjunct tagmemes with the GM Purposive, the filler commences with *for* (the purpose of) or *in order to* or these may be substituted or inserted, e.g.,

> Joe went out *for some cigarettes*,
> Joe went out *to get some cigarettes*.

(4) The tagmeme in which it occurs need not be filled by noun phrase constructions having as filler of the head tagmeme a noun or pronoun representing an animate being or institution.

6.3. Diagnostic matrix for Grammatical Meanings

	Anim.	Subj. Active	Subj. Passive	Obj.	Comp.	*by* Ad.	*for* Ad.	*with* Ad.	*to* Ad.	Dir. Ad.
aff.	±		+	+						
ag	+	+				+				
ben-i	+	+	+	+	+		+			
ben-o	+						+			
ben-fo	+						+			
fact	±		+	+					+	
inst	±	+	+	+		+		+		
loc-i	±	+	+	+					+	+
loc-o										
loc-fo										
neut	±	+	+	+	+					
part	+	+	+	+		+				
purp	±							+		

	Loc. Ad.	Cl. Perm.	Imp. Test	WHAT DO test	Ag. only	BE v-ing test	As only overt GM with loc-i	As only overt GM	Occ. with same GM	Ag. must be implied
aff.					+		+	+		
ag			+	+	+	+	+	+		
ben-i										
ben-o					+					+
ben-fo		+			+					+
fact					+			+		
inst			+		+	+	+	+		
loc-i	+				+		+		+	
loc-o	+				+					+
loc-fo	+	+			+					
neut					+		+		+	
part			+		+	+	+	+		
purp					+					

The symbol + indicates that the criterion is positively diagnostic, and the symbol ± indicates that the criterion is not diagnostic.

6.3.1. *Notes on headings of diagnostic matrix*

The following notes explain the abbreviated headings in the preceding diagnostic matrix:

Anim.   The Head tagmeme of the noun phrase which serves as a filler to a tagmeme with the indicated GM, must be filled by a noun or pronoun representing an animate being or institution of animate beings.

Subj. Active   The GM occurs as the Subject of a predicate filler in the Active Voice.

Subj. Passive   The GM occurs in a Subject tagmeme with a co-occurring Predicate tagmeme which contains a verbal filler in the Passive Voice.

Obj.   The GM occurs in an Object tagmeme.

Comp.   The GM occurs in a Complement tagmeme.

by Ad.   The GM occurs in an Adjunct tagmeme, whose filler commences with *by*.

for Ad.   The GM occurs in an Adjunct tagmeme, whose filler commences with *for*.

with Ad.   The GM occurs in an Adjunct tagmeme, whose filler commences with *with*.

to Ad.   The GM occurs in an Adjunct tagmeme, whose filler commences with *to*.

Dir. Ad.   The GM may occur in an Adjunct tagmeme, whose filler commences with a directional preposition such as: to, into, from, towards (not only with a restricted subset of such prepositions).

Loc. Ad.   The GM may occur in an Adjunct tagmeme, whose filler commences with a locational preposition such as: in, on, under, behind (not only with a restricted subset of such prepositions).

Cl. Perm.   If the GM occurs in an Adjunct tagmeme, this is freely permutable between clause initial and clause final position.

Imp. Test   The GM may occur in a 'deleted Subject tagmeme' of an Imperative Clause.

WHAT DO test   The GM may occur in the position X in

WHAT X DO to Y BE Z ...

This test works freely with the GM Agentive. Some readers/listeners will also accept Instruments as in: *What the plough did to the land was turn it.* but others would consider this unacceptable.

Ag. only   The GM may occur in a clause construction with no other *overt* GM than Agentive.

BE v-ing test   The GM may occur in a Subject tagmeme of a clause construction where the verbal filler of the Predicate tagmeme is in the BE v-ing form. This is always the case where the Subject tagmeme has the GM Agentive, but some readers/listeners will accept Subject tagmemes with the GM Instrumental into this frame, at least in some instances, e.g.,

> That medicine is curing him.

With the GM Participative, such verb forms do occur, but usually only when some time is specified or implied as in:

> Jack is enjoying his work nowadays,
> Fred is fearing the consequences (of the action he took).

As only overt GM with loc-i   May occur in a clause with no other overt GM than loc-i. Thus:

> $+ S_{ag}$: Fred   + P: walked $+ Ad_{loc-i}$: to town.

> $+ S_{aff}$: The parcel   + P: was sent $+ Ad_{loc-i}$: to Adelaide.

> $+ S_{part}$: Jim   + P: was sent $+ Ad_{loc-i}$: to town.

As only overt GM   May occur as the only overt GM at clause level within a clause.
Occurring with same GM   May co-occur at clause level with the same GM.
Ag. must be implied   May only occur if the GM, Agentive is implied, even if not actually overt.

7. SOME ENGLISH PREDICATE FILLERS AND THEIR GRAMMATICAL FORM AND MEANING IMPLICATIONS

7.0. Introduction

In this chapter, a selection of English Predicate fillers will be examined in the light of the previous discussion. For each Predicate filler, a formula will first be given indicating the GM implications of that filler. Each GM will be preceded by + or ±, according to whether the GM is always implied or whether it is optional. Thus, with *give*, Agentive (ag) should be indicated with + unless, of course, we are considering special meanings of *give*, such as

> These cows give a lot of milk,
> This soil gives very poor crops.

It would seem more appropriate to consider these meanings of *give* as related to those of *yield*. Thus, a lexicon might have an entry such as:

> GIVE (2) — see YIELD.

Although a common meaning of *give* would always imply the GM Agentive, this GM would not be overtly indicated in a Passive Clause such as

> Tom was given a book.

Similarly, *give* implies the GM Participative or Benefactive, but the latter is not always overt as, for example, in

> Mrs. Green gives very generously,

where we may be considering Mrs. Green's donations to a charity, or

Mary gave five dollars,

where we are discussing how much various people gave towards a fund. It will be noticed that we cannot normally have overt manifestations of the GMs, Benefactive or Participative as Objects unless either Affective or Neutral is also overt. Thus, we do not have

Jack gave Mary,

with the sense of Mary being the recipient of a gift. However, we can have the Participative GM occurring as an Adjunct without any overt Neutral of Affective GM if the head of the filler of the Participative Adjunct is a noun such as: *charities, the poor, the needy*. Thus, we have

Mrs. Green gives to the poor,

but not normally

Jack gives to Mary.

Thus we can see that in a fuller description we need to consider the fillers of Clause Level tagmemes. Thus, in this instance, it is not simply that the Head needs to be a noun representing a *class* of people or an institution. We can have

Mrs. Green gave to a beggar.

It would seem that when what is given is not overt, the Head of the filler of the Benefactive tagmeme needs to be 'a person or institution worthy of being helped'.

After the formula of GMs examples will be given of the occurrences of these GMs with various Grammatical Forms (GFs), that is with Subject, Object, Complement or Adjunct. Then, examples will be given of the various GF–GM relationships co-occurring with other GF–GM relationships. Thus, with *give*, Subject$_{agentive}$ co-occurs with Object$_{benefactive}$ and Object$_{affective}$.

As mentioned earlier, the fillers of Predicate tagmemes have a strong influence on the existence and co-occurrence of certain GMs in a clause construction as well as GM–GF relationships. A grouping together of Predicate fillers according to their 'potentiality' is thus of interest and will be further discussed in ch. 8, e.g., Predicate fillers which may co-occur with only Affective and Agentive GMs in Subject, Object, Complement and Adjunct tagmemes will be grouped together and examined to see whether they may co-occur. Thus, *learn* and *examine* which may both have Subject$_{agentive}$ and Object$_{neutral}$ should be able to co-occur as in

Henry examined and learned the contents of the book,

as long as the Object filler is of such a nature that it may be examined and learned. Of course, fillers of Object tagmemes with different GMs may some-times co-occur, as with Factitive and Affective, in the case of *build* as long as Factitive precedes Affective. Thus, we could have:

Jones built and destroyed his own house,

but they may not occur in the reverse order if we are referring to the same house. Even with *build* and *destroy,* the co-occurrence possibilities seem to be more restricted than with *learn* and *examine.* Thus

Jones built and destroyed the house,

sounds strange unless there is emphasis on *and.* On the other hand, *hit* and *slap* would seem to co-occur more freely as in

Mrs. Brown hit and slapped her disobedient child.

In general, it would seem that the more differences in GM, the less likeli-hood there is of two Predicate fillers being co-ordinated with *and* although they may both co-occur with the same GFs, e.g., Subject and Object. Thus

Bloggs robbed and feared Smith,

where *rob* would co-occur with Subject$_{agentive}$ and Object$_{participative}$ and *fear* would co-occur with Subject$_{participative}$ and Object$_{neutral}$.

7.1. Grammatical Meaning implications of Predicate fillers
In the following P (the Predicate) has been omitted but always occurs after the Subject tagmeme.

7.1.1. *Open (also close, shut, lock)*
GM implications +aff ±ag ±inst.

Examples of GM–GF co-occurrence

S_{aff} *The door* opened.
S_{ag} *Tom* opened the door.
S_{inst} *The key* opened the door.
O_{aff} Tom opened *the door.*
Ad_{ag} The door was opened *by Tom.*
Ad_{inst} The door was opened *with a key.*

Possible overt configurations of GF and GM

$+S_{aff}$	The door opened.
	The door was opened.
$+S_{ag} + O_{aff}$	Tom opened the door.
$+S_{inst} + O_{aff}$	The key opened the door.
$+S_{aff} + Ad_{ag}$	The door was opened by Tom.
$+S_{aff} + Ad_{inst}$	The door was opened with a key.
	The door opened with a key.
$+S_{ag} + O_{aff} + Ad_{inst}$	Tom opened the door with a key.
$+S_{aff} + Ad_{ag} + Ad_{inst}$	The door was opened by Tom with a key.

It will be noticed that the GM, Affective is always overt and an obligatory GM in the above formula. It is interesting that GM Agentive is only optional although present (if only covert) in many instances. In the construction *the door opened* no overt agent is present and no covert agent need be implied. In a case like this, the presupposition to the statement could have been a faulty catch. In the passive construction *the door was opened* it is different – a covert agent is always implied.

It is felt that in constructions featuring GM Instrumental, a covert agent is in most cases implied; e.g.,

The key opened the door

implies that somebody must have turned it in the lock.

7.1.2. *Cook (also bake)*

The following two variant formulae can be established for the GM implications of

cook   (also of *bake*)

| I | + aff ± ag |
| II | + fact + ag ± ben-i |

Related verbs like: *stew, fry, boil* do not seem to have quite the same GM implications. They do not seem to imply Factitive as an alternative to Affective. Thus, although we can have: *I'll cook you a dinner* and *I'll bake you a cake* where there are no related sentences of the type: **What I'll do to the dinner is cook it* or **What I'll do to the cake is bake it,* this is not so with stew, fry and boil:

> What I'll do to the chops is stew them,
> What I'll do to the potatoes is boil them,

are semantically possible constructions. Furthermore, although we can have inner Benefactives with *cook, bake, fry* and *boil* as may be seen in: *I'll cook you a dinner, I'll bake you a cake, I'll fry/boil you an egg,* fewer native speakers would seem to accept: *I'll stew you some chops.*

It may be doubted whether ben-i may occur as Subject with *cook* and *bake*. A bland sentence such as *Joe was cooked a meal* may appear unacceptable whereas *When we visited the Smiths, we were cooked a delicious meal by Mary* would seem to be acceptable. Therefore, I would consider that one may have an inner Benefactive Subject.

Examples of GM–GF co-occurrence

S_{aff}	*The chicken* is cooking.
	The chicken was cooked.
S_{ag}	*Mary* cooked the chicken.
S_{ben-i}	*I* was cooked a delicious meal by Mary
S_{fact}	*The meal* was cooked by Mary.
O_{aff}	Mary cooked *the chicken.*
O_{ben-i}	Mary cooked *me* a meal.
O_{fact}	Mary cooked *a meal.*
Ad_{ag}	The meal was cooked *by Mary.*
Ad_{ben-i}	Mary cooked a meal *for me.*

Possible overt configurations of GF and GM

$+S_{aff}$	The chicken is cooking.
	The chicken was cooked.
$+S_{ag}$	Mary is cooking.
$+S_{fact}$	The meal is cooking.

$+S_{fact} + Ad_{ag}$ The chicken was cooked by Mary.
$+S_{ag} + O_{aff}$ Mary cooked the chicken.
$+S_{ag} + O_{fact}$ Mary cooked the meal.
$+S_{ben-i} + O_{fact}$ I was cooked a meal.
$+S_{fact} + Ad_{ag}$ The meal was cooked by Mary.
$+S_{ag} + O_{fact} + Ad_{ben-i}$ Mary cooked a meal for me.
$+S_{ag} + O_{ben-i} + O_{fact}$ Mary cooked me a meal.
$+S_{ben-i} + O_{fact} + Ad_{ag}$ I was cooked a meal by Mary.
$+S_{fact} + Ad_{ben-i} + Ad_{ag}$ A meal was cooked for me by Mary.

7.1.3. See (also notice, find, discover)
GM implications + neut + part

Examples of GM–GF co-occurrence
S_{neut} *The boy* was seen.
S_{part} *Jim* saw the boy.
O_{neut} Jim saw *the boy.*
Ad_{part} The boy was seen *by Jim.*

Possible overt configurations of GF and GM
$+S_{neut}$ The boy was seen.
$+S_{neut} + Ad_{part}$ The boy was seen by Jim.
$+S_{part} + O_{neut}$ Jim saw the boy.

It should be made clear at this stage that conventions of GM implications do not necessarily mean that a GM with a + symbol needs to be overtly manifested in a tagmeme in every construction. The + symbol in these implications does, however, stipulate that the GM in question, if not overtly present, is always implied.

This is apparent in the example

The boy was seen.

Here, the covert Participative is implied, i.e. some *animate being* (the one who does the seeing) is involved.

7.1.4. Show
GM implications + neut + part ± ag

Examples of GM–GF co-occurrence

S_{ag}	*Mary* showed the picture to Joan.
S_{neut}	*The picture* was shown to Joan.
S_{part}	*Joan* was shown the picture.
O_{neut}	Mary showed *the picture* to Joan.
O_{part}	Mary showed *Joan* the picture.
Ad_{ag}	The picture was shown to Joan *by Mary*.
Ad_{part}	The picture was shown *to Joan* by Mary.

Possible overt configurations of GF and GM

$+S_{neut}$	Your slip is showing.
	The picture was shown.
$+S_{ag} + O_{neut}$	Mary showed the picture.
$+S_{neut} + Ad_{ag}$	The picture was shown by Mary.
$+S_{neut} + Ad_{part}$	The picture was shown to Joan.
$+S_{part} + O_{neut}$	Joan was shown the picture.
$+S_{ag} + O_{part} + O_{neut}$	Mary showed Joan the picture.
$+S_{ag} + O_{neut} + Ad_{part}$	Mary showed the picture to Joan.
$+S_{neut} + Ad_{part} + Ad_{ag}$	The picture was shown to Joan by Mary.
$+S_{part} + O_{neut} + Ad_{ag}$	Joan was shown the picture by Mary.

It can be seen that the Agentive is again not an obligatory GM. At first sight, one could argue that constructions such as

The picture was shown,

do imply a covert GM Agentive, i.e. someone *does* the showing, but one must consider such examples as

Your slip is showing,

where no intentional exhibition is intended by the wearer. In both cases, however, the Participative is covertly present.

It seems, however, that the GM Participative can only be overtly manifested in a clause construction tagmeme, if the GM Agentive is present (either overtly or covertly); i.e. it is possible to say

I was shown the document by Mr. McTavish,
The document was shown to me (by Mr. McTavish),

but not
> *Your slip is showing *to me*.

It may be mentioned that *exhibit* has similar GM implications, although the GM Agentive is always implied. The GF possibilities, however, are not quite the same. We do not have

> *Mary exhibited Joan the picture,

or

> *Joan was exhibited the picture (by Mary).

7.1.5. *Kill (also exterminate, injure, shoot)*
GM implications + ag + inst + part

Examples of GM–GF co-occurrence

S_{ag}	*Bloggs* killed Sykes.
S_{inst}	*A bullet* killed Sykes.
S_{part}	*Sykes* was killed.
O_{part}	Bloggs killed *Sykes*.
Ad_{ag}	Sykes was killed *by Bloggs*.
Ad_{inst}	Sykes was killed *with a bullet*.

Possible overt configurations of GF and GM

$+S_{ag}$	Bloggs killed.
$+S_{inst}$	This bullet killed.
$+S_{part}$	Sykes was killed.
$+S_{ag} + O_{part}$	Bloggs killed Sykes.
$+S_{ag} + Ad_{inst}$	Bloggs killed with this pistol.
$+S_{inst} + O_{part}$	This pistol killed Sykes.
$+S_{part} + Ad_{ag}$	Sykes was killed by Bloggs.
$+S_{part} + Ad_{inst}$	Bloggs was killed with this pistol.
$+S_{ag} + O_{part} + Ad_{inst}$	Bloggs killed Sykes with this pistol.
$+S_{part} + Ad_{ag} + Ad_{inst}$	Sykes was killed by Bloggs with this pistol.

7.1.6. *Murder (also execute, assassinate)*
GM implications + ag + inst + part

The GM implications for *murder* are the same as for *kill* but there is quite a variation in their GM–GF occurrence; i.e. in constructions where the Predicate filler is *murder* and is present in an active form, the GM Agentive must be overtly present in the Subject tagmeme. It cannot be replaced by GM Instrumental, e.g.,

> Bloggs murdered Sykes,

but not

> *A bullet murdered Sykes.

If the verbal Predicate filler is *kill*, the GM Instrumental may appear in Subject tagmemes, e.g.,

> This knife killed old Murgatroyd.

Examples of GM–GF co-occurrence

S_{ag}	*Bloggs* murdered Sykes.
S_{part}	*Sykes* was murdered.
O_{part}	Bloggs murdered *Sykes.*
Ad_{inst}	Bloggs murdered Sykes *with a pistol.*

Possible overt configurations of GF and GM

$+S_{ag}$	Bloggs murdered. (For example as a statement of the way Bloggs gained his income.)
$+S_{part}$	Sykes was murdered.
$+S_{ag} + O_{part}$	Bloggs murdered Sykes.
$+S_{ag} + Ad_{inst}$	Bloggs murdered with a pistol. (For example in answer to a question about *how* Bloggs carried out his murders.)
$+S_{part} + Ad_{ag}$	Sykes was murdered by Bloggs.
$+S_{part} + Ad_{inst}$	Sykes was murdered with a pistol.
$+S_{ag} + O_{part} + Ad_{inst}$	Bloggs murdered Sykes with a pistol.
$+S_{part} + Ad_{ag} + Ad_{inst}$	Sykes was murdered by Bloggs with a pistol.

In the case of *execute* and *assassinate*, the differences seem to be mainly related to Aspect D. Thus, the person executed is one who is (or is supposed to be according to his executioners) guilty of a crime and the person assassinated is always in some way an important figure, although not necessarily a head of state, e.g., Gandhi.

7.1.7. *Know*
GM implications + neut + part

Examples of GM-GF co-occurrence

S_{neut} *That man* is known.
S_{part} *Jim* knows that man.
Ad_{part} That man is known *by/to Jim.*

Possible overt configurations of GF and GM

$+S_{neut}$ That man is known.
$+S_{neut} + Ad_{part}$ That man is known by/to Jim.
$+S_{part} + O_{neut}$ Jim knows that man.

This is a case where the entity which is known (whether animate or in-animate) is expressed by the GM Neutral and not by the GM Affective as it is in no way affected by the mental state of knowing expressed by the verbal filler of the Predicate tagmeme.

An Affective test (e.g., the WHAT DO test) would not be possible here, e.g.,

*What I did to the man was know him.

7.1.8. *Learn*
GM Implications + ag/part [1] + neut

Examples of GM–GF co-occurrence

$S_{ag/part}$ *Fred* learned the lesson.
S_{neut} *The lesson* was learned by Fred.
$Ad_{ag/part}$ The lesson was learned *by Fred.*

Possible overt configurations of GF and GM

$+S_{ag} + O_{neut} (+S_{part} + O_{neut})$ Fred learned the lesson.
$+S_{neut}$ The lesson was learned.
$+S_{neut} + Ad_{ag} (+S_{neut} + Ad_{part})$ The lesson was learned by Fred.

Fillmore (1968a:31) suggests the following case frame for learn $(+[\_O +A])$. The choice of Agentive only for the 'learner' seems a far too simplistic approach to this problem. Many educationalists and psychologists may even completely reject the idea of an 'agent' (i.e. an instigator of the action) being involved in the learning process. Some theories of learning suggest rather a kind of absorption process by the 'learner' – this would strongly suggest the GM Participative.

[1] The following convention is sued to show that either one of two GMs may occur, but not both: Z/Y.

Examples such as these would confirm the suggested GM:

(a)   After staying for two years in Ongobongoland, Mrs Peterson found that she had learnt the language despite her antagonistic attitude towards it,

(b)   The little white mice learned to use the treadmill,

(c)   He has certainly learned his lesson!
        (meaning he has had an unpleasant experience which taught him something),

(d)   Mrs. Bloggs learned that her husband had been arrested.

The GM Agentive would certainly be impossible in the last case. By applying the Imperative test the following strange order would be obtained (order to Mrs. Bloggs):

Learn that your husband has been arrested!

In spite of these examples, there exist however quite a number of constructions where the GM Agentive *is* present, e.g.,

Mary, learn your vocabulary!

One may be influenced in one's decisions by modern theories (e.g., the theory of learning) but the fact remains that language reflects also generally held view points. In many instances *learn* is used with the concept of 'learn by heart', 'take in' or 'make an effort to acquire knowledge'.

It appears to me that the general concept of *learn* is *acquire knowledge* but that it can also have the concept *attempt to acquire knowledge*. I suggest that in the latter case, one of the GMs present is Agentive, whereas in the former case it is Participative.

7.1.9. *Look at* (also *examine, view, peruse*)
GM implications + ag + neut ± inst

Examples of GM–GF co-occurrence
S_{ag} *Jack* looked at the picture.
S_{neut} *The picture* was looked at by Jack.

O_{neut} Jack looked at *the picture.*
Ad_{ag} The picture was looked at *by Jack.*
Ad_{inst} Jack looked at the picture *with a magnifying glass.*

Possible overt configurations of GF and GM

$+S_{neut}$	The picture was looked at.
$+S_{ag} + O_{neut}$	Jack looked at the picture.
$+S_{neut} + Ad_{ag}$	The picture was looked at by Jack.
$+S_{neut} + Ad_{inst}$	The picture was looked at with a magnifying glass.
$+S_{ag} + O_{neut} + Ad_{inst}$	Jack looked at the picture with a magnifying glass.
$+S_{neut} + Ad_{ag} + Ad_{inst}$	The picture was looked at by Jack with a magnifying glass.
	The picture was looked at with a magnifying glass by Jack.

As can be notices, the Predicate filler considered above is *looked at* not just *look*. I class these two as different concepts. *Look at* has close affinity with such fillers as *examine, view, peruse,* i.e. they cannot occur in clause constructions where apart from the Predicate tagmeme there is only a Subject tagmeme with the GM Agentive, e.g.,

> *Jack looked at,
> *Jack viewed.

Look, on the other hand, can appear in such a configuration, e.g.,

> John looked.

A further difference between the GM implications of the fillers *look at* and *look* is that the former is usually connected with Object tagmemes with the GM Neutral, e.g.,

> Aunt Aggie looked at *the ormolu clock,*

which would be a response to the question

> *What* did Aunt Aggie look at (do)?

whereas the latter is usually connected with Adjunct tagmemes with the GM loc-i, e.g.,

> Jack looked *towards the island,*

which would be a response to the question

> Where (in what direction) did Jack look?

7.1.10. *Give*
GM implication + ag + aff/neut + ben-i/part

Examples of GM–GF co-occurrence

S_{ag}	*Jean* gave the book to Edna.
S_{aff}	*The book* was given to Edna.
S_{neut}	*The house* was given to Mary.
S_{ben-i}	*Mary* was given a house.
S_{part}	*Tom* was given a spade (so that he could dig).
O_{aff}	Jean gave *the book* to Edna.
O_{ben-i}	Jean gave *Edna* the book.
O_{neut}	Mr. Black gave Mary *a house.*
O_{part}	The foreman gave *Tom* a spade.
Ad_{ag}	Edna was given the book *by Jean.*
Ad_{ben-i}	The book was given *to Edna.*
Ad_{part}	The spade was given *to Tom* by the foreman.

Possible overt configurations of GF and GM

$+S_{aff}$	A book was given.
$+S_{ag}$	Mrs. Green gave.
$+S_{neut}$	A block of land was given.
$+S_{ag} + O_{aff}$	Mrs. Green gave $5.
$+S_{ag} + O_{neut}$	Mrs. Green gave a block of land.
$+S_{ag} + Ad_{ben-i}$	Mrs. Green gave to the poor.
$+S_{aff} + Ad_{ag}$	$5 were given by Mrs. Green.
$+S_{aff} + Ad_{ben-i}$	$5 were given to the poor.
$+S_{aff} + Ad_{part}$	A spade was given to Tom (and he was told to start digging).
$+S_{neut} + Ad_{ag}$	A block of land was given by Mr. Green.
$+S_{neut} + Ad_{ben-i}$	A block of land was given to Mary.
$+S_{neut} + Ad_{part}$	The assignment was given to Tom.

$+S_{ben\text{-}i} + O_{aff}$	The poor were given \$5.
$+S_{ben\text{-}i} + O_{neut}$	Mary was given a block of land.
$+S_{part} + O_{aff}$	Tom was given a spade.
$+S_{part} + O_{neut}$	Tom was given the assignment.
$+S_{aff} + Ad_{ben\text{-}i} + Ad_{ag}$	A book was given to Edna by Jean
$+S_{aff} + Ad_{part} + Ad_{ag}$	A spade was given to Tom by the foreman.
$+S_{ag} + O_{aff} + Ad_{ben\text{-}i}$	Jean gave a book to Edna.
$+S_{ag} + O_{aff} + Ad_{part}$	The foreman gave a spade to Tom.
$+S_{ag} + O_{ben\text{-}i} + O_{aff}$	Jean gave Edna a book.
$+S_{ag} + O_{part} + O_{aff}$	The foreman gave Tom a spade.
$+S_{ag} + O_{neut} + Ad_{ben\text{-}i}$	Mr. Green gave a block of land to Mary.
$+S_{ag} + O_{neut} + Ad_{part}$	The manager gave the assignment to Tom.
$+S_{ag} + O_{ben\text{-}i} + O_{neut}$	Mr. Green gave Mary a block of land.
$+S_{ag} + O_{part} + O_{neut}$	The manager gave Tom the assignment.
$+S_{ben\text{-}i} + O_{aff} + Ad_{ag}$	Edna was given a book by Jean.
$+S_{ben\text{-}i} + O_{neut} + Ad_{ag}$	Mary was given a block of land by Mr. Green.
$+S_{neut} + Ad_{ben\text{-}i} + Ad_{ag}$	A block of land was given to Mary by Mr. Green.
$+S_{neut} + Ad_{part} + Ad_{ag}$	The assignment was given to Tom by the Manager.
$+S_{part} + O_{aff} + Ad_{ag}$	Tom was given the spade by the foreman.
$+S_{part} + O_{neut} + Ad_{ag}$	Tom was given the assignment by the manager.

With this Predicate filler, two GMs which are mutually exclusive but where one of them must appear are GM ben-i and GM part. In cases where there is a change of ownership, GM ben-i is present, e.g.,

>   Mary was given a house,

in other cases GM part is manifested, e.g.,

>   Tom (the handyman) was given a spade
>   (so that he could dig over the garden).

One identification test would be the substitution of 'make a gift of' for 'give'.

>   Mary was *made a gift of* a house

but Tom was just handed the spade for a short period.

7.1.11. *Send*
GM Implications +ag +aff +loc-i/part

Examples of GM–GF co-occurrence
S_{ag} *Bill* sent the parcel to Betty.
S_{aff} *The parcel* was sent to Betty.
S_{part} *Betty* was sent a parcel.
O_{aff} Bill sent *the parcel* to Betty.
O_{part} Bill sent *Betty* a parcel.
Ad_{ag} The parcel was sent *by Bill.*
Ad_{loc-i} Bill sent a parcel *to Sydney*
Ad_{part} Bill sent a parcel *to Betty*

Possible overt configurations of GF and GM
$+S_{aff}$ A parcel was sent.
$+S_{aff} + Ad_{ag}$ A parcel was sent by Bill.
$+S_{aff} + Ad_{part}$ A parcel was sent to Betty.
$+S_{aff} + Ad_{loc-i}$ A parcel was sent to Sydney.
$+S_{ag} + O_{aff}$ Bill sent a parcel.
$+S_{part} + O_{aff}$ Betty was sent a parcel.
$+S_{aff} + Ad_{loc-i} + Ad_{ag}$ A parcel was sent to Sydney by Bill.
$+S_{aff} + Ad_{part} + Ad_{ag}$ A parcel was sent to Betty by Bill.
$+S_{ag} + O_{aff} + Ad_{part}$ Bill sent a parcel to Betty.
$+S_{ag} + O_{part} + O_{aff}$ Bill sent Betty a parcel.
$+S_{ag} + O_{aff} + O_{loc-i}$ Bill sent a parcel to Sydney.
$+S_{part} + O_{aff} + Ad_{ag}$ Betty was sent a parcel by Bill.

It will be noticed that loc-i does not occur as Subject or Object; clauses such as: *Bill sent Sydney a parcel* (where Sydney is the name of a city) do not occur. There is, of course, the case of constructions such as

We'll send Melbourne a copy of this contract.

However, in this context *Melbourne* does not really refer to the city as such but rather to

'The people in our Melbourne office',

or

'Our Melbourne manager'.

7.1.12. *Donate*
GM implications + ag + aff/neut + ben-i

Examples of GM–GF co-occurrence

S_{ag} *Lord Cholmondley* donated some books to the library.
S_{aff} *A gold watch* was donated to Jones.
S_{neut} *A block of land* was donated to the school.
O_{aff} The company donated *a gold watch* to Jones.
O_{neut} Lord Cholmondley donated *a block of land* to the school.
Ad_{ben-i} Lord Cholmondley donated a block of land *to the school.*

Possible overt configurations of GF and GM

$+ S_{aff}$	A gold watch was donated.
$+ S_{neut}$	A block of land was donated.
$+ S_{aff} + Ad_{ag}$	A gold watch was donated by the company.
$+ S_{aff} + Ad_{ben-i}$	A gold watch was donated to Jones.
$+ S_{ag} + O_{aff}$	The company donated a gold watch.
$+ S_{ag} + O_{neut}$	Lord Cholmondley donated a block of land.
$+ S_{ag} + Ad_{ben-i}$	Mary donated to the fund. (This only seems possible if the ben-i tagmeme is filled by a noun phrase having as its head a noun representing some institution.)
$+ S_{neut} + Ad_{ag}$	A block of land was donated by Lord Cholmondley.
$+ S_{neut} + Ad_{ben-i}$	A block of land was donated to the school.
$+ S_{aff} + Ad_{ben-i} + Ad_{ag}$	A gold watch was donated to Jones.
$+ S_{ag} + O_{aff} + Ad_{ben-i}$	The company donated a gold watch to Jones
$+ S_{ag} + O_{neut} + Ad_{ben-i}$	Lord Cholmondley donated a block of land to the school.
$+ S_{neut} + Ad_{ben-i} + Ad_{ag}$	A block of land was donated to the school by Lord Cholmondley.

7.1.13. *Like (also enjoy, admire, dislike, detest)*
GM implications + neut + part

Examples of GM–GF co-occurrence

S_{neut}	*The meal* was liked by everyone.
S_{part}	*Everyone* liked the meal.
O_{neut}	Everyone liked *the meal.*
Ad_{part}	The meal was liked *by everyone.*

Possible overt configurations of GF and GM

$+S_{neut}$	The meal was liked.
$+S_{neut} + Ad_{part}$	The meal was liked by everyone.
$+S_{part} + O_{neut}$	Everyone liked the meal.

In cases such as *like* where emotive concepts are concerned, there is no GM Agentive present. A WHAT DO test would not be appropriate, e.g.,

*What he did to the meal was like it.

Equally strange would be an order to someone:

*Like that meal!

7.1.14. *Smear (also splash, daub, plaster, paint)*
GM implications + ag + inst + loc-i

Examples of GM–GF co-occurrence

S_{ag}	*Joe* smeared paint on the wall.
S_{inst}	*Paint* was smeared on the wall.
S_{loc-i}	*The wall* was smeared with paint.
O_{inst}	Joe smeared *paint* on the wall.
O_{loc-i}	Joe smeared *the wall* with paint.
Ad_{ag}	The wall was smeared with paint *by Joe.*
Ad_{inst}	Joe smeared the wall *with paint.*
Ad_{loc-i}	Joe smeared paint *on the wall.*

Possible overt configurations of GF and GM

$+S_{loc-i}$	The wall was smeared.
$+S_{ag} + O_{loc-i}$	Joe smeared the wall.
$+S_{inst} + Ad_{loc-i}$	Paint was smeared on the wall.
$+S_{loc-i} + Ad_{inst}$	The wall was smeared with paint.
$+S_{loc-i} + Ad_{ag}$	The wall was smeared by Joe.
$+S_{ag} + O_{loc-i} + Ad_{inst}$	Joe smeared the wall with paint.
$+S_{ag} + O_{inst} + Ad_{loc-i}$	Joe smeared paint on the wall.
$+S_{inst} + Ad_{loc-i} + Ad_{ag}$	Paint was smeared on the wall by Joe.
$+S_{loc-i} + Ad_{inst} + Ad_{ag}$	The wall was smeared with paint by Joe.

With most of these verbs, the Instrumental tagmeme may have as the head of its noun phrase either a material like *paint, kalsomine, mud* or an instrument for applying the material such as a *brush*. Also, as *paint* usually implies the application of paint, the Instrumental filler is more likely to be an instrument for application. Otherwise, it is likely to be a sub-variety of paint, such as enamel or a brand name.

7.1.15. Break (also smash, shatter)
GM implications + aff ± ag ± inst

Examples of GM–GF co-occurrence

S_{aff}	*The vase* broke.
	The vase was broken.
S_{ag}	*Jim* broke the vase.
S_{inst}	*The hammer* broke the vase.
O_{aff}	Jim broke *the vase*.
Ad_{ag}	The vase was broken *by Jim*.
Ad_{inst}	The vase was broken *with a hammer*.

Possible overt configurations of GF and GM

$+ S_{aff}$	The vase broke.
	The vase was broken.
$+ S_{aff} + Ad_{ag}$	The vase was broken by Jim.
$+ S_{aff} + Ad_{inst}$	The vase was broken with a hammer.
$+ S_{ag} + O_{aff}$	Jim broke the vase.
$+ S_{inst} + O_{aff}$	The hammer broke the vase.
$+ S_{aff} + Ad_{ag} + Ad_{inst}$	The vase was broken by Jim with a hammer.
$+ S_{ag} + O_{aff} + Ad_{inst}$	Jim broke the vase with a hammer.

With these verbs, an Affective Subject may co-occur with a verb in the Active Voice, and without any Agent or Instrument.

7.1.16. Hit (also slap, smack, strike, bash, etc.)
GM implications + ag + aff/part + inst

Examples of GM–GF co-occurrence

S_{ag}	*Fred* hit the table.
S_{aff}	*The table* was hit.
S_{part}	*Claude* was hit.
	Claude was hit *in the nose*.
S_{inst}	*The bullet* hit.
O_{aff}	Fred hit *the table*.

O_{part} Fred hit *Claude (in the nose)*.
Ad_{ag} Claude was hit *by Fred*.
Ad_{inst} Claude was hit *(by a bullet, with a whip)*.

Possible overt configurations of GF and GM

$+S_{aff}$	The table was hit.
$+S_{inst}$	The bullet hit.
$+S_{part}$	Claude was hit (in the nose).
$+S_{aff} + Ad_{ag}$	The table was hit by Fred.
$+S_{aff} + Ad_{inst}$	The table was hit by a bullet/with a hammer.
$+S_{ag} + O_{aff}$	Fred hit the table.
$+S_{ag} + O_{part}$	Fred hit Claude.
$+S_{part} + Ad_{ag}$	Claude was hit by Fred.
$+S_{part} + Ad_{inst}$	Claude was hit by a bullet/with a whip.
$+S_{aff} + Ad_{inst} + Ad_{ag}$	The table was hit with a hammer by Fred.
$+S_{ag} + O_{aff} + Ad_{inst}$	Fred hit the table with a hammer.
$+S_{ag} + O_{part} + Ad_{inst}$	Fred hit Claude with a hammer.
$+S_{part} + Ad_{inst} + Ad_{ag}$	Claude was hit with a whip by Fred.

7.1.17. *Rob (also defraud, swindle – with slight variation in the Affective tagmeme preposition)*

GM implications   +ag   +part   +aff

Examples of GM–GF co-occurrence

S_{ag}	*Robin Hood* robbed the rich.
S_{part}	*The rich* were robbed by Robin Hood.
O_{part}	Robin Hood robbed *the rich*.
Ad_{ag}	The rich were robbed *by Robin Hood*.
Ad_{aff}	Robin Hood robbed the rich *of their money*.

Possible overt configurations of GF and GM

$+S_{ag}$	Robin Hood robbed.
$+S_{part}$	The rich were robbed.
$+S_{ag} + O_{part}$	Robin Hood robbed the rich.
$+S_{part} + Ad_{ag}$	The rich were robbed by Robin Hood.
$+S_{ag} + O_{part} + Ad_{aff}$	Robin Hood robbed the rich of their money.
$+S_{part} + Ad_{aff} + Ad_{ag}$	The rich were robbed of their money by Robin Hood.

With *swindle* the filler of the Adjunct with the GM Affective commences with *out of*, as in

> Bloggs swindled Oggs out of $100.

7.1.18. *Steal*
GM implications + ag + aff + part

Examples of GM–GF co-occurrence
S_{aff}	*Money* was stolen from Smith.
S_{ag}	*Bloggs* steals.
O_{aff}	Bloggs stole *money*.
Ad_{ag}	The money was stolen *by Bloggs*.
Ad_{part}	The money was stolen *from Smith*.

Possible overt configurations of GF and GM
$\dot{+}S_{aff}$	The money was stolen.
$+S_{ag}$	Bloggs stole.
$+S_{aff} + Ad_{ag}$	The money was stolen by Bloggs.
$+S_{aff} + Ad_{part}$	The money was stolen from Smith.
$+S_{ag} + O_{aff}$	Bloggs stole the money.
$+S_{ag} + Ad_{part}$	Bloggs stole from Smith.
$+S_{aff} + Ad_{part} + Ad_{ag}$	The money was stolen from Smith by Bloggs.
$+S_{ag} + O_{aff} + Ad_{part}$	Bloggs stole the money from Smith.

Although *steal* would seem to have the same GM implications as the verbs in 7.1.17, the combinations of GF and GM are rather different. The GM Affective is implied with both verbal concepts but in clause constructions with *rob*, its manifestations are extremely restricted, i.e. it can only appear in Adjunct tagmemes (see 7.1.17) e.g.,

> Robin Hood robbed the rich *of their money*.

In clause constructions, however, which contain the Predicate filler *steal*, GM Affective can appear in Subject and Object tagmemes (but *not* in Adjunct tagmemes):

> Bloggs stole *money*.

As far as the GM Participative is concerned, the matter seems to be reversed. In clause constructions where *rob* is the Predicate filler, GM Participative appears in Subject or Object (but *not* Adjunct) tagmemes (see 7.1.17):

> *The rich* were robbed by Robin Hood,
> Robin Hood robbed *the rich* of their money,

not

> *Robin Hood robbed from the rich,

whereas in clause constructions with the verbal filler *steal*, the GM Participative *only* appears in Adjunct tagmemes, e.g.,

> Bloggs stole money *from his employer.*

Fillmore (1968b:388) has made similar observations.

7.1.19. *Buy (also purchase)*
GM implications + ag + neut + part ± ben-i

Examples of GM–GF co-occurrence

S_{ag}	*Sam* bought a book.
S_{neut}	*A book* was bought by Sam.
S_{ben-i}	*Lucy* was bought a book.
O_{ben-i}	Sam bought *Lucy* a book.
O_{neut}	Sam bought *a book.*
Ad_{ag}	A book was bought *by Sam.*
Ad_{ben-i}	Sam bought a book *for Lucy.*
Ad_{part}	Sam bought a book *from Black & Co.*

Possible overt configurations of GF and GM

$+ S_{neut}$	A book was bought.
$+ S_{ag} + O_{neut}$	Sam bought a book.
$+ S_{ag} + Ad_{part}$	Sam bought from Black & Co.
$+ S_{neut} + Ad_{ag}$	A book was bought by Sam.
$+ S_{neut} + Ad_{ben-i}$	A book was bought for Lucy.
$+ S_{neut} + Ad_{part}$	A book was bought from Black & Co.
$+ S_{ag} + O_{ben-i} + O_{neut}$	Sam bought Lucy a book. (unlikely with *purchase*)
$+ S_{ag} + O_{neut} + Ad_{ben-i}$	Sam bought a book for Lucy.
$+ S_{ag} + O_{neut} + Ad_{part}$	Sam bought a book from Black & Co.
$+ S_{ben-i} + O_{neut} + Ad_{ag}$	Lucy was bought a book by Sam.
$+ S_{ben-i} + O_{neut} + Ad_{part}$	Lucy was bought a book from Black & Co.

$+S_{neut} + Ad_{ben-i} + Ad_{ag}$	A book was bought for Lucy by Sam
$+S_{neut} + Ad_{ag} + Ad_{part}$	A book was bought by Sam from Black & Co.
$+S_{ag} + O_{neut} + Ad_{ben-i} + Ad_{part}$	Sam bought a book for Lucy from Black & Co.
$+S_{ag} + O_{ben-i} + O_{neut} + Ad_{part}$	Sam bought Lucy a book from Black & Co.
$+S_{ben-i} + O_{neut} + Ad_{ag} + Ad_{part}$	Lucy was bought a book by Sam from Black & Co.
$+S_{neut} + Ad_{ben-i} + Ad_{ag} + Ad_{part}$	A book was bought for Lucy by Sam from Black & Co.

7.1.20. *Sell*
GM implications $+ag$ $+neut$ $+part$

Examples of GM–GF co-occurrence

S_{ag}	*Black & Co* sold a book.
S_{neut}	*A book* was sold by Black & Co.
S_{part}	*Sam* was sold a book.
O_{neut}	Black & Co. sold *a book*.
O_{part}	Black & Co. sold *Sam* a book.
Ad_{ag}	A book was sold *by Black & Co*.
Ad_{part}	A book was sold *to Sam*.

Possible overt configurations of GF and GM

$+S_{neut}$	A book was sold.
	This book is selling.
$+S_{ag} + O_{neut}$	Black & Co. sold a book.
$+S_{ag} + Ad_{part}$	Black & Co. sold to Sam.
$+S_{neut} + Ad_{ag}$	A book was sold by Black & Co.
$+S_{neut} + Ad_{part}$	A book was sold to Sam.
	The book sold to Sam.
$+S_{ag} + O_{part} + O_{neut}$	Black & Co. sold Sam a book.
$+S_{part} + O_{neut} + Ad_{ag}$	A book was sold to Sam by Black & Co.

This verb, unlike those in 7.1.19 does not co-occur with inner Benefactives.

7.1.21. *Please (also charm, delight)*
GM implications $+ (+ag \pm inst)/neut$ $+part$

Examples of GM–GF co-occurrence

S_{ag}	*Tom* pleased Mary with/by his tricks.
S_{inst}	*Tom's tricks* pleased Mary.
S_{neut}	*The scenery* pleased Mary.
S_{part}	*Mary* was pleased by/with Tom's tricks.
Ad_{ag}	Mary was pleased *by Tom.*
Ad_{inst}	Mary was pleased *by/with Tom's tricks.*
Ad_{neut}	Mary was pleased *with the scenery.*

Possible overt configurations of GF and GM

$+S_{inst}$	Tom's tricks pleased.
$+S_{neut}$	The scenery pleased.
$+S_{part}$	Mary was pleased.
$+S_{ag} + O_{part}$	Tom pleased Mary.
$+S_{ag} + Ad_{inst}$	Tom pleased with his tricks
$+S_{inst} + O_{part}$	Tom's tricks pleased Mary.
$+S_{neut} + O_{part}$	The scenery pleased Mary.
$+S_{part} + Ad_{ag}$	Mary was pleased by Tom.
$+S_{part} + Ad_{inst}$	Mary was pleased by/with Tom's tricks.
$+S_{part} + Ad_{neut}$	Mary was pleased with the scenery.
$+S_{ag} + O_{part} + Ad_{inst}$	Tom pleased Mary with his tricks.
$+S_{part} + Ad_{ag} + Ad_{inst}$	Mary was pleased by Tom with his tricks.

The GM implications of these Predicate fillers are of a more complex nature. The GM Participative (e.g., the being who receives pleasure) is always implied but the second obligatory GM could be either an Agentive, e.g.,

> *Count Ferrozi* charmed Mrs. Murgatroyd.

(In this case the GM Instrumental is optional: e.g.,

> Bobo, the clown, delighted the children *with his tricks*),

or the second obligatory GM could be a Neutral (in this case no GM Instrumental is possible):

> *The view from our bedroom window* delighted us.

7.1.22. Rent (e.g., a house from someone) (also borrow)
GM implications + ag + neut + part

Examples of GM–GF co-occurrence

S_{ag}	*Henry* rents the house from Victor.
S_{neut}	*The house* is rented from Victor.
O_{neut}	Henry rents *the house* from Victor.
Ad_{ag}	The house is rented *by Henry*.
Ad_{part}	The house is rented *from Victor*.

Possible overt configurations of GF and GM

$+ S_{neut}$	The house is rented.
$+ S_{ag} + O_{neut}$	Henry rents the house.
$+ S_{ag} + Ad_{part}$	Henry rents from Victor.
$+ S_{neut} + Ad_{ag}$	The house is rented by Henry.
$+ S_{neut} + Ad_{part}$	The house is rented from Victor.
$+ S_{ag} + O_{neut} + Ad_{part}$	Henry rents the house from Victor.
$+ S_{neut} + Ad_{part} + Ad_{ag}$	The house is rented from Victor by Henry.

Although the GM Participative is obligatory in the implications of these Predicate fillers, its manifestations are restricted to Adjunct tagmemes only (see examples above). This holds for Australian and British-English usage, where the entity expressed by GM Agentive is the tenant or prospective tenant. In some varieties of English, this is not so and constructions such as

He'll rent me a room,

and

He'll rent some rooms out to the students,

are common (see 7.1.23). In my variety of English, the verbal filler 'let' would be used in these cases.

7.1.23. Let (e.g., a house to someone) (also rent, if used this way and lend)
GM implications + ag + neut + part

Examples of GM–GF co-occurrence

S_{ag}	*Victor* lets his house to Henry.
S_{neut}	*The house* is let to Henry.
O_{neut}	Victor lets *his house*.
Ad_{ag}	The house is let *by Victor*.
Ad_{part}	The house is let *to Henry*.

Possible overt configurations of GF and GM

$+S_{neut}$	The house is let.
$+S_{ag} + O_{neut}$	Victor lets his house.
$+S_{neut} + Ad_{ag}$	The house is let by Victor.
$+S_{neut} + Ad_{part}$	The house is let to Henry.
$+S_{ag} + O_{neut} + Ad_{part}$	Victor lets his house to Henry.
$+S_{neut} + Ad_{part} + Ad_{ag}$	The house is let to Henry by Victor.

7.1.24. *Resemble (also look like)*
GM implications + neut + neut

Examples of GM–GF co-occurrence

S_{neut}	*Jack* resembles his brother.
C_{neut}	Jack resembles *his brother.*

Possible overt configurations of GF and GM

$+S_{neut} + C_{neut}$	Jack resembles his brother.

7.1.25. *Smell*
GM implications + neut ± ag/part

Examples of GM–GF co-occurrence

S_{ag}	*Joan* smelt the meat (she sniffed at it purposely to see whether it was fresh)
S_{neut}	*The meat* was smelt.
	The meat smells.
S_{part}	*Joan* smelt the meat. (she noticed the smell without purposely trying to do so.)
O_{neut}	Joan smelt *the meat.*
Ad_{ag}	The meat was smelt *by Joan.*
Ad_{part}	The meat was smelt *by everyone.*

Possible overt configurations of GF and GM

$+S_{neut}$	The meat was smelt (sniffed at).
	The meat smelt.
$+S_{ag} + O_{neut}$	Joan smelt the meat.
$+S_{neut} + Ad_{ag}$	The meat was smelt by Joan.
$+S_{neut} + Ad_{part}$	The meat was smelt by Joan.
$+S_{part} + O_{neut}$	Joan smelt the meat.

7.1.26. *Change (also turn)*
GM implications $+$ aff $+$ fact $\pm$ (ag $\pm$ inst)

Examples of GM–GF co-occurrence

S_{aff}	*The liquid* changed (in)to gas.
	The liquid was changed into gas.
S_{ag}	*Jones* changed the liquid into gas.
S_{inst}	*This device* changes the liquid into gas.
O_{aff}	Jones changed *the liquid* into gas.
Ad_{ag}	The liquid was changed into gas *by Jones.*
Ad_{fact}	The liquid changed *into gas*
Ad_{inst}	The liquid was changed into gas *by/with this device.*

Possible overt configurations of GF and GM

$+S_{aff}+Ad_{fact}$	The liquid changed into gas.
	The liquid was changed into gas.
$+S_{aff}+Ad_{fact}+Ad_{ag}$	The liquid was changed into gas by Jones.
$+S_{aff}+Ad_{fact}+Ad_{inst}$	The liquid was changed into gas with/by this device.
	The liquid changed into gas with/by means of this device.
$+S_{ag}+O_{aff}+Ad_{fact}$	Jones changed the liquid into gas.
$+S_{ag}+O_{aff}+Ad_{fact}+Ad_{inst}$	Jones changed the liquid into gas with this instrument.
$+S_{aff}+Ad_{fact}+Ad_{inst}+Ad_{ag}$	The liquid was changed into gas with this instrument by Jones.

Because of the unilateral direction of these processes, the initial stage, as expressed by GM Affective co-occurs only with GF Subject and Object, the second stage, expressed by GM Factitive, occurs only with GF Adjunct. As Adjunct tagmemes in English commonly occur towards the end of clause constructions after Subject and Object tagmemes, we can observe here the unilateral direction of the GM relation guided by a corresponding GF relation.

The GM Agentive is optional but the optional GM Instrumental is dependent on the presence of a GM Agentive, even if it is only covert.

7.1.27. *Have*
GM implications. With *have* (and also with *be,* as will be shown in 7.1.28) there are so many possible GM implications and such varied configurations of GF and GM that it would seem preferable to consider various GM combinations separately.

+ ag + aff ± loc-i (*have*, with similar meaning to *take*)

S_{ag} *Joe* had a biscuit.

C_{aff} Joe had *a biscuit*.

$Ad_{loc\text{-}i}$ Joe had a biscuit *from the tin*.

Possible overt configurations of GF and GM

$+ S_{ag} + C_{aff}$ Joe had a biscuit.

$+ S \quad + C \quad + Ad$ Joe had a biscuit from the tin.

+ ag + neut + loc-i (*have*, with similar meaning to *keep*)

S_{ag} *Joe* has the car in the garage.

C_{neut} Joe has *the car* in the garage.

$Ad_{loc\text{-}i}$ Joe has the car *in the garage*.

Possible overt configurations of GF and GM

$+ S_{ag} + C_{neut} + Ad_{loc\text{-}i}$ Joe has the car in the garage.

+ part + neut (*have* with the sense of Inalienable Possession)

S_{part} *Mary* has red hair.

C_{neut} Mary has *red hair*.

Possible overt configurations of GF and GM

$+ S_{part} + C_{neut}$ Mary has red hair.

+ben-i + part (Alienable Possession, also *own*, *possess*)

$S_{ben\text{-}i}$ *Tom* has a car.

C_{neut} Tom has *a car*.

Possible overt configurations of GF and GM

$+ S_{ben\text{-}i} + C_{neut}$ Tom has a car.

+ loc-i + neut (*have* with the sense of a location having)

$S_{loc\text{-}i}$ *Melbourne* has tall buildings.

C_{neut} Melbourne has *tall buildings*.

Possible overt configurations of GF and GM

$+ S_{loc\text{-}i} + C_{neut}$ Melbourne has tall buildings.

+ loc-i + aff (*have* with the sense of conceptually temporary location)

$S_{loc\text{-}i}$ *The box* has toys in it.

C_{aff} The box has *toys* in it.
Ad_{loc-i} The box has toys *in it.*

Possible overt configurations of GF and GM
   $+S_{loc-i} + C_{aff} + Ad_{loc-i}$ The box has toys in it.

7.1.28. *Be*
+part +loc-i (with the sense of a person being somewhere)
   S_{part} *Joe* is at his office.
   Ad_{loc-i} Joe is *at his office.*

Possible overt configurations of GF and GM
   $+S_{part} + Ad_{loc-i}$ Joe is at his office.

+ben-i +neut (Alienable Possession)
   S_{ben-i} *Jim's* is the red book.
   C_{neut} Jim's is *the red book.*

Possible overt configurations of GF and GM
   $+S_{ben-i} + C_{neut}$ Jim's is the red book.

+neut +loc-i (general or permanent location of something)
   S_{neut} There is *a red roof* on that house.
   Ad_{loc-i} There is a red roof *on that house.*

Possible overt configurations of GF and GM
   $+S_{neut} + Ad_{loc-i}$ There is a red roof on that house.

+aff +loc-i (temporary location)
   S_{aff} *The toys* are in the box.
   Ad_{loc-i} The toys are *in the box.*

Possible overt configurations of GF and GM
   $+S_{aff} + Ad_{loc-i}$ The toys are in the box.

7.1.29. *Be happy (also, be miserable, be sad, be uneasy, etc.)*
GM implications +part ±neut
   S_{part} *Jim* is happy.
   Ad_{neut} Jim is happy *about his success.*

Possible overt configurations of GF and GM

$+S_{part}$	Jim is happy.
$+S_{part} + Ad_{neut}$	Jim is happy about his success.

7.1.30. *Be nasty (also be unpleasant, be helpful, be vicious, be kind)*
GM implications + neut/+ ag + part

S_{ag}	*Joe* is being nasty.
S_{neut}	*That medicine* is nasty.
	Joe is nasty. (He is not being nasty, it is a statement about him as he appears to the speaker/writer.)
Ad_{part}	Joe is (being) nasty *to his sister.*

Possible overt configurations of GF and GM

$+S_{ag}$	Joe is being nasty.
$+S_{neut}$	That medicine is nasty.
$+S_{ag} + Ad_{part}$	Joe is (being) nasty to his sister.

We do not have combinations of the GMs Neutral + Participative with these Predicate fillers, e.g.,

*That medicine is nasty to me.

8. OVERT GRAMMATICAL MEANINGS AND THEIR GRAMMATICAL FORMS

8.0. Grammatical Form and Grammatical Meaning correlations

In this chapter, it will be considered which Predicate fillers of those previously discussed may co-occur with various correlations of GF and GM. For example, what Predicate fillers may co-occur with Subject $_{affective}$ and with no other GM manifested as Object, Complement or Adjunct? Furthermore, it will be useful to subdivide those Predicate fillers which may occur in the Active Voice and those which may occur in the Passive Voice in such an environment. Therefore, I shall commence with occurrences of Predicate fillers in the active voice and with only one overt GM, appearing in a Subject tagmeme. These occurrences will be subdivided into the various GMs. After this, I shall consider co-occurrences of two GMs and so on and then deal with Passive constructions in the same way.

A fairly stringent test of conjoinability which will be applied here is the conjoining of two Predicate tagmemes in a clause construction with *and.* This precludes the repetition of any other tagmeme in the construction as well as the Predicate tagmeme. The reason for this is that a wide variety of verbal fillers could be conjoined in the following way:

> Mary loved the dress and (she) bought it,

whereas

> *Mary loved and bought the dress,

sounds strange for reasons that will be discussed later in this chapter.

8.1. Group 1: Predicate fillers in Active Voice; one overt GM

Subgroup 1a: $+S_{aff}$: open, close, shut, lock, cook, bake, break, smash, shatter.

Any restriction on conjoinability of these verbs stems from a lack of correspondence or partial lack of correspondence of the D-aspect of the Subject tagmemes, e.g. entities whose D-aspect (lexical meaning) enables them to *open, close, shut* or *lock* often cannot *cook* or *bake,* e.g.,

> *The door opened and cooked.

However, there are instances where this is feasible, e.g.,

> The substance baked and opened in the intense heat.

The conjoining of *open* and *lock,* although unusual, is possible, e.g. something can lock in an open position.

Subgroup 1b: $+S_{ag}$: cook, kill, murder, give, rob, steal, be nasty.

The apparently 'odd' items in the preceding list would seem to be: *cook* and *give.* The reason why these last two verbal fillers are not easily joined to the rest lies in the variation of implied GMs. The importance of GMs which are not always overtly manifested must not be overlooked. The table in appendix A shows that unlike the rest of the above group, *cook* has no Participative implication. When *give* appears in clause constructions without Object tagmemes, it has Benefactive implication (see appendix A) which none of the other verbal fillers of the group has under these conditions.

Subgroup 1c: $+S_{fact}$: cook (also bake).

These two may conjoin as in: *The meal was cooking and baking.* However, this is unusual, as normally one verb or the other would be selected.

Subgroup 1d: $+S_{inst}$: kill, hit, please.

Again, there is a lack of correspondence of the D-aspect of the Subject tagmemes which would appear in constructions with *kill* and *hit* on the one hand and *please* on the other, e.g.,

> *The bullet hit and pleased,
> *The scenery pleased and killed.

Subgroup 1e: $+ S_{neut}$: sell, please, smell, be nasty.

Except for *please* and *be nasty* where the D-aspects show considerable opposition, the Predicate fillers above are as a rule conjoinable, e.g.,

> That meat is nasty and smells,
> This product pleases and sells well.

Subgroup 1f: $+ S_{part}$: be happy

8.2. Matrix showing the degrees of conjoinability with *and* within group 1

Subgroups to which this conjoinability applies are indicated in the matrix. (Specific order of fillers in conjoining process has not been taken into consideration.)

Symbols used in matrix

xx readily conjoinable.

o less easily conjoinable because of differences in implied GMs.

- less easily conjoinable because of close similarity or because of opposition or partial opposition within the D-aspects of the Predicate fillers themselves.

x less easily conjoinable because of lack of or partial lack of correspondence in the D-aspects of the subject tagmemes which usually co-occur with these Predicate fillers.

Subgroups appearing in matrix

1a $+ S_{aff}$
1b $+ S_{ag}$
1c $+ S_{fact}$
1d $+ S_{inst}$
1e $+ S_{neut}$

8.3. Group 2: Predicate fillers in Active Voice; two overt GMs

Subgroup 2a: open, cook, give, send, donate, break, hit, steal.

Conjoinability is impeded in several cases because of different GM implications. *Send* and *steal* have Participative implications and *give* and *donate* have Benefactive implications. In addition, there is a close similarity in the D-aspects of *give* and *donate*.

Subgroup 2b: $+ S_{ag} + O_{fact}$: cook.

This would conjoin with *bake* in the case that something needed to be

Matrix showing the degrees of conjoinability with *and* within group 1.

	bake	be nasty	break	close	cook	give	hit	kill	murder	lock	open	please	rob	sell	shatter	shut	smash	smell	steal
bake			xx a	x a	xx abc					x a	x a				x a		x a		
be nasty				o b		o b		xx b	xx b			- e	xx b	xx e				xx e	xx b
break	xx a			xx a	xx a					xx a	xx a				- a				
close	x a		xx a		x a					xx a	xx a				xx a	- a	xx a		
cook	xx abc	o b	xx a	x a				o b	o b	x a	x a	o b			x a		x a		o b
give		o b						o b	o b				o b						o b
hit								xx d				x d							
kill		xx b		o b	o b	xx d			xx b			x d	xx b						xx b
murder		xx b		o b	o b			xx b					xx b						xx b
lock	x a		xx a	xx a	x a						xx a				xx a		xx a		
open	x a		xx a	xx a	x a					xx a					xx a	xx a	xx a		
please		- e					x d	x d						xx e					
rob		xx b			o b	o b		xx b	xx b										- b
sell		xx e										xx e							
shatter	x a		- a	xx a	x a					xx a	xx a						xx a	- a	
shut	x a		xx a	- a						xx a					xx a		xx a		
smash	x a		xx a	x a						xx a	xx a				- a	xx a			
smell		xx e												xx e					
steal		xx b		o b	o b			xx b	xx b				- b						

cooked and then baked. It would not conjoin with a verb like *build* which implies the Factitive as there usually is a lack or partial lack of correspondence between the D-aspects of their co-occurring Object tagmemes.

Subgroup 2c: $+S_{ag} + O_{neut}$: show, learn, look at, give, donate, buy, sell, rent, let, smell.

Here again, there are some restrictions because of aspect D of the Predicate fillers themselves as well as the D-aspects of co-occurring Object tagmemes. In addition, *show, buy, sell, rent* and *let* are verbs which imply the GM Participative and *give* [1] and *donate* imply the GM Benefactive. Therefore these Predicate fillers do not seem to conjoin freely with *learn, look at* and *smell.* Although there is an opposition in the D-aspects of *buy* and *sell,* these fillers are conjoinable in constructions such as

He buys and sells second-hand furniture,

where consecutiveness is implied.

Subgroup 2d: $+S_{ag} + O_{loc-i}$: smear (splash, daub, plaster, paint).
These verbs all seem conjoinable, e.g.,

He plastered and painted the wall.

Subgroup 2e: $+S_{ag} + O_{part}$: kill, murder, hit, rob, please.
Normally, *kill,* and *murder* would not be conjoined because of similarity in their D-aspect. Again, *please* varies considerably in its D-aspect from the others. Therefore conjoining is less likely.

Subgroup 2f: $+S_{inst} + O_{aff}$: open, break, hit.
These would seem to be conjoinable, e.g.,

The axe hit, broke and opened the box.

Subgroup 2g: $+S_{inst} + O_{part}$: kill, hit, please.
Here, *please* is unlikely to co-occur with the other two because of aspect D features. The first two are conjoinable as in:

The bullet hit and killed him.

[1] It appears that in constructions where *give* is co-occurring with a Subject tagmeme or a Subject tagmeme and either $Object_{neutral}$ or $Object_{affective}$, it always has Benefactive implications.

Subgroup 2h: $+S_{neut} + O_{part}$: please.
Other verbs which could conjoin are: *delight, intrigue, fascinate* and with a 'negative' sense: *frighten, disgust, repel.*

Subgroup 2j: $+S_{part} + O_{neut}$: see, know, like, smell.
These would seem to be conjoinable.

Subgroup 2k: $+S_{aff} + Ad_{inst}$: open.

Subgroup 2l: $+S_{aff} + Ad_{loc-i}$: be.

Subgroup 2m: $+S_{aff} + Ad_{fact}$: change.
Conjoinable with similar verbs like: *grow* as in

  The seedling grew and changed into a fine tree.

Subgroup 2n: $+S_{ag} + Ad_{ben-i}$: give, donate.

Subgroup 2o: $+S_{ag} + Ad_{inst}$: kill, murder, please.
Aspect D features would make it unlikely that these would be conjoined.

Subgroup 2p: $+S_{ag} + Ad_{part}$: steal (from), buy (from), sell (to), rent (from), be nasty (to).
The main restrictions on conjoinability seem to be the differences in prepositions. There are also aspect D restrictions. However, we can have:

  Joe is nasty to his neighbour and steals from him.

Subgroup 2q: $+S_{ag} + C_{aff}$: have.

Subgroup 2r: $+S_{ben-i} + C_{neut}$: be, have.
Because the filler of the Subject tagmeme must be in the possessive form with *be* we cannot have direct conjoining but sentences of the type:

  Jim's is the red book and he's had it for years.

Subgroup 2s: $+S_{loc-i} + C_{neut}$: have.

Subgroup 2t: $+S_{neut} + Ad_{loc-i}$: (there) be.

Subgroup 2u: $+ S_{neut} + Ad_{part}$: sell.

Subgroup 2v: $+ S_{neut} + C_{neut}$: resemble.

Subgroup 2w: $+ S_{part} + Ad_{loc-i}$: be.

Subgroup 2x: $+ S_{part} + Ad_{neut}$: be happy (about).

Subgroup 2y: $+ S_{part} + C_{neut}$: have (Inalienable Possession).

8.4. Matrix showing the degrees of conjoinability with *and* within group 2

Subgroups to which this conjoinability applies are indicated in the matrix. (Specific order of fillers in conjoining process has not been taken into account.)

Symbols used in the matrix
(Often only one symbol is shown in the matrix, this does not mean that only one factor need be responsible for the particular degree of conjoinability; often more than one are involved. I have chosen the factor that appeared to play the main part.)
xx readily conjoinable.
o less easily conjoinable because of difference in implied GMs.
ox less easily conjoinable because of lack of correspondence in the filler form (C-aspect) of the co-occurring Adjunct tagmemes.
－ unlikely to conjoin because of close similarity or because of opposition or partial opposition within the D-aspects of the Predicate fillers themselves.
x less easily conjoinable because of lack of or partial lack of correspondence in the D-aspect of the Object tagmemes which usually co-occur with these Predicate fillers.

Subgroups appearing in matrix

2a	$+ S_{ag} + O_{aff}$	2h	$+ S_{neut} + O_{part}$
2b	$+ S_{ag} + O_{fact}$	2j	$+ S_{part} + O_{neut}$
2c	$+ S_{ag} + O_{neut}$	2m	$+ S_{aff} + Ad_{fact}$
2d	$+ S_{ag} + O_{loc-i}$	2n	$+ S_{ag} + Ad_{ben-i}$
2e	$+ S_{ag} + O_{part}$	2o	$+ S_{ag} + Ad_{inst}$
2f	$+ S_{inst} + O_{aff}$	2p	$+ S_{ag} + Ad_{part}$
2g	$+ S_{inst} + O_{part}$		

Matrix showing the degrees of conjoinability with *and* within group 2

	bake	be nasty	break	build	buy	change	cook	delight	donate	give	grow	hit	kill	know	murder	learn
bake							xx b									
be nasty					ox p											
break							xx a		o a	o a		xx af				
build	x b															
buy		ox p							o c	o c						o c
change											xx m					
cook	xx b		xx a	x b					o a	o a		x a				
delight																
donate			o a			o c	o a			− ac		o a				o c
give			o a			o c	o a		− acn			o a				o c
grow						xx m										
hit			xx af				x a		o a	o a			xx eg		xx e	
kill												xx eg			− eo	
know																
murder												xx e	− eo			
learn					o c				o c	o c						
let					xx c				o c	o c						o c
like														xx j		
look at					o c				o c	o c						xx c
open			xx af				xx a		o a	o a		xx af				
paint																
plaster																
please								xx h				− eg	− ego		− eo	
rent		ox p			xx cp				o c	o c						o c
rob															xx e	
see														xx j		
sell					xx c				o c	o c						o c
send			o a				o a		o a	o a		o a				
show					− c				o c	o c						o c
smell					o c				o c	o c				xx j		x c
steal		ox p	o a		xx p		o a		o a	o a		o a				

Matrix showing the degrees of conjoinability with *and* within group 2 (*continued*)

	let	like	look at	open	paint	plaster	please	rent	rob	see	sell	send	show	smell	steal
bake															
be nasty								ox p							ox p
break			xx af										o a		o a
build															
buy	xx c		o c					xx cp			xx c		– c	o c	
change															
cook			xx a								o a				o a
delight							xx h								
donate	o c		o c	o a				o c			o c		o a	o c	o a
give	o c		o c	o a				o c			o c	o a	o a	o c	o a
grow															
hit			xx af					– eg							o a
kill								– ego	xx e				o a		
know		xx j								xx j				xx j	
murder								– eo	xx e						
learn	o c		xx c					o c			o c		o c	x c	
let			o c					– c			xx c		xx c		
like										xx j				xx j	
look at	o c							o c			o c		o c	xx c	
open											xx a				xx a
paint						xx d									
plaster					xx d										
please								– e							
rent	– c		o c								– c			o c	– p
rob							– e								
see		xx j												xx j	
sell	xx c		o c					xx c					xx c	o c	ox p
send			xx a												– a
show	xx c		o c					– c			xx c			o c	
smell	o c	xx j	xx c					o c		xx j	o c		o c		
steal				xx a				– p			ox p	– a			

8.5. Group 3: Predicate fillers in Active Voice; three overt GMs
Subgroup 3a: $+ S_{aff} + Ad_{fact} + Ad_{inst}$: change, turn.

Subgroup 3b: $+ S_{ag} + O_{aff} + Ad_{inst}$: open, break (smash, shatter), hit.
These seem to be conjoinable, e.g.,

Tom hit, smashed and opened the door with an axe.

Subgroup 3c: $+ S_{ag} + O_{aff} + Ad_{ben-i}$: give, donate.
These would not normally be conjoined because of the similarity in their D-aspects.

Subgroup 3d: $+ S_{ag} + O_{aff} + Ad_{part}$: give, send, steal.
Similarity or opposition within the D-aspect make conjoining of these fillers less likely. There is also a lack of correspondence between the C-aspects of the co-occurring Adjunct tagmemes.

Subgroup 3e: $+ S_{ag} + O_{aff} + Ad_{loc-i}$: send.

Subgroup 3f: $+ S_{ag} + O_{aff} + Ad_{fact}$: change (turn).

Subgroup 3g: $+ S_{ag} + C_{neut} + Ad_{loc-i}$: have.

Subgroup 3h: $+ S_{ag} + O_{ben-i} + O_{aff}$: cook.

Subgroup 3j: $+ S_{ag} + O_{ben-i} + O_{aff}$: give.

Subgroup 3k: $+ S_{ag} + O_{ben-i} + O_{neut}$: give, buy.

Subgroup 3l: $+ S_{ag} + O_{fact} + Ad_{ben-i}$: cook.

Subgroup 3m: $+ S_{ag} + O_{inst} + Ad_{loc-i}$: smear (splash, daub, plaster, paint).
All of these seem to be joinable.

Subgroup 3n: $+ S_{ag} + O_{loc-i} + Ad_{inst}$: smear (splash, daub, plaster, paint).

Subgroup 3o: $+ S_{ag} + O_{neut} + Ad_{inst}$: look at (examine, view, peruse).

Subgroup 3p: $+ S_{ag} + O_{neut} + Ad_{ben-i}$: give (to), donate (to), buy (for).
Restrictions on *and* conjoinability would be because of a lack of corre-

spondence in the Filler Form (C-aspect) of the co-occurring Adjunct tagmemes (i.e. different prepositions) but we can have:

I bought a block of land for Mary and gave it to her.

Subgroup 3q: $+S_{ag} + O_{neut} + Ad_{part}$: give (to), show (to), buy (from), sell (to), rent (from), let (to).
Restrictions on conjoinability would be because of aspect D, and because of the differences in the C-aspect of the co-occurring Adjunct tagmemes.

Subgroup 3r: $+S_{ag} + O_{aff} + Ad_{loc-i}$: have.

Subgroup 3s: $+S_{ag} + O_{part} + O_{neut}$: show, sell, give.

Subgroup 3t: $+S_{ag} + O_{part} + Ad_{inst}$: kill, murder, hit (slap, smack, strike, bash), please.
Here, *please* would not co-occur because of aspect D differences.

Subgroup 3u: $+S_{ag} + O_{part} + O_{aff}$: give, send.

Subgroup 3v: $+S_{ag} + O_{part} + Ad_{aff}$: rob.

Subgroup 3w: $+S_{inst} + O_{aff} + Ad_{fact}$: change (turn).

Subgroup 3x: $+S_{loc-i} + C_{aff} + Ad_{loc-i}$: have.

(e.g.   *The box has toys in it.*)

8.6. Matrix showing the degrees of conjoinability with *and* within group 3

Subgroups to which this conjoinability applies are indicated in the matrix. (Specific order of fillers in the conjoining process has not been taken into account.)

Symbols used in matrix
xx readily conjoinable.
x less easily conjoinable because of lack or partial lack of correspondence in the D-aspect of the object-tagmemes which usually co-occur with these Predicate fillers.
ox less easily conjoinable because of lack of correspondence in the Filler Form (C-aspect) of the co-occurring Adjunct tagmeme.
o Less easily conjoinable because of close similarity or opposition (or partial opposition) within the D-aspects of the Predicate fillers themselves.

Matrix showing the degrees of conjoinability with *and* within group 3

	break	buy	change	donate	examine	give	hit	kill	let	look at	murder	open	plaster	please	rent	sell	send	show	smear	steal	turn
break						xx b̄						xx b̄									
buy			ox p		xx kp				ox q						xx q	ox q		ox q			
change																					− afw
donate		ox p				− cp															
examine											xx o										
give		xx kp		− cp					− q						ox q	− qs	− du	xx qs		− d	
hit	xx b̄								xx t		xx t	xx b̄		= t							
kill							xx t				− t			− t							
let		ox q				= q									ox q	xx q		xx q			
look at				xx o																	
murder							xx t	− t						− t							
open	xx b̄					xx b̄															
plaster																			xx mn		
please							− t	− t			− t										
rent		ox q				ox q			ox q									ox q			
sell		ox q				− qs			xx q						ox q			xx qs			
send				− du																	
show		ox q				xx qs			xx q						ox q	xx qs					
smear													xx mn								
steal																					
turn			− af w																		

Subgroups appearing in matrix

3a	$+S_{aff} + Ad_{fac} + Ad_{inst}$		3o	$+S_{ag} + O_{neut} + Ad_{inst}$
3b	$+S_{ag} + O_{aff} + Ad_{inst}$		3p	$+S_{ag} + O_{neut} + Ad_{ben-i}$
3c	$+S_{ag} + O_{aff} + Ad_{ben-i}$		3q	$+S_{ag} + O_{neut} + Ad_{part}$
3d	$+S_{ag} + O_{aff} + Ad_{part}$		3s	$+S_{ag} + O_{part} + O_{neut}$
3f	$+S_{ag} + O_{aff} + Ad_{fact}$		3t	$+S_{ag} + O_{part} + Ad_{inst}$
3k	$+S_{ag} + O_{ben-i} + O_{neut}$		3u	$+S_{ag} + O_{part} + O_{aff}$
3m	$+S_{ag} + O_{inst} + Ad_{loc-i}$		3w	$+S_{inst} + O_{aff} + Ad_{fact}$
3n	$+S_{ag} + O_{loc-i} + Ad_{inst}$			

8.7. Group 4: Predicate fillers in Active Voice; four overt GMs

Subgroup 4a: $+S_{ag} + O_{aff} + Ad_{fact} + Ad_{inst}$: change (turn).

Subgroup 4b: $+S_{ag} + O_{ben-i} + O_{neut} + Ad_{part}$: buy.

Subgroup 4c: $+S_{ag} + O_{neut} + Ad_{ben-i} + Ad_{part}$: buy.

8.8. Group P1: Predicate fillers in Passive Voice; one over GM

Subgroup P1a: $+S_{aff}$: open, cook, give, send, donate, break (smash, shatter), hit, steal.
These all seem to be conjoinable, within the restrictions imposed by aspect D.

Subgroup P1b: $+S_{loc-i}$: smear (splash, daub, plaster, paint).

Subgroup P1c: $+S_{neut}$: see, show, know, learn, look at, give, donate, like, buy, (purchase), sell, rent, let, smell.
These all seem to be conjoinable, within the restrictions imposed by aspect D.

Subgroup P1d: $+S_{fact}$: cook (bake).
If we try to conjoin an Affective Subject and a Factitive Subject with this verb we obtain an unacceptable sentence like

The chicken and a meal were cooked.

Subgroup P1e: $+S_{part}$: kill, murder, hit, rob (defraud, swindle), please charm, delight).
Here again, the only restrictions on conjoinability seem to be because the last three show a considerable variation in their D-aspect to the rest of the subgroup.

8.9. Group P2: Predicate fillers in Passive Voice; two overt GMs

Subgroup P2a: $+S_{aff} + Ad_{ag}$: open, cook, give, send, donate, break (smash, shatter), hit, steal.

These would seem to be conjoinable.

Subgroup P2b: $+S_{aff} + Ad_{ben-i}$: give, donate.

These would not normally be conjoined because of close similarities in meaning.

Subgroup P2c: $+S_{aff} + Ad_{fact}$: change (turn).

Subgroup P2d: $+S_{aff} + Ad_{inst}$: open, break (smash, shatter), hit.

These seem to be conjoinable.

Subgroup P2e: $+S_{aff} + Ad_{loc-i}$: send.

Subgroup P2f: $+S_{aff} + Ad_{part}$: give, send, steal.

Here again, *steal* would not be as readily conjoinable because of the different preposition. However, we may have *The book was given to and then stolen from Fred.* We can also see that Participative and Locative Adjuncts may not be combined if we consider **The book was sent to Fred and New York.*

Subgroup P2g: $+S_{ben-i} + O_{aff}$: give.

Subgroup P2h: $+S_{ben-i} + O_{fact}$: cook (bake).

Subgroup P2j: $+S_{ben-i} + O_{neut}$: give.

Subgroup P2k: $+S_{fact} + Ad_{ag}$: cook (bake).

Subgroup P2l: $+S_{fact} + Ad_{ben-i}$: cook (bake).

Subgroup P2m: $+S_{inst} + Ad_{loc-i}$: smear (splash, daub, plaster, paint).

Subgroup P2n: $+S_{loc-i} + Ad_{ag}$: smear (splash, daub, plaster, paint).

Subgroup P2o: $+S_{loc-i} + Ad_{inst}$: smear (splash, daub, plaster, paint).

Subgroup P2p: $+S_{neut} + Ad_{ag}$: show, learn, look at (examine, view, peruse), give, donate, buy (purchase), sell, rent, borrow, let, smell.

Some of these are not readily conjoinable because of aspect D features. Furthermore, *learn, look at, examine, view, peruse, smell* are not verbs which imply the Participative GM in addition to Agentive in the way that the others do.

Subgroup P2q: $+ S_{neut} + Ad_{ben-i}$: give, donate, buy.
There is a difference in the C-aspect of the co-occurring Adjunct tagmemes which restricts conjoinability, e.g.,

> Money was given *to the poor*

but

> A new dress was bought *for Agatha.*

Subgroup P2r: $+ S_{neut} + Ad_{inst}$: look at (examine, view, peruse).

Subgroup P2s: $+ S_{neut} + Ad_{part}$: (a) see (notice, find, discover), know, like, smell + by; (b) give, let, show, sell + to; (c) rent, borrow, buy (purchase) + from.
Within each set of fillers above, there seems to be conjoinability but the difference in the C-aspect of co-occurring Adjunct tagmemes makes conjoining between the first set and the others impossible. The first set also consists of verbs in which no Agentive GM is implied whereas with the other two sets Agentive is implied.

Subgroup P2t: $+ S_{part} + Ad_{ag}$: kill, murder, hit (slap, smack, strike, bash), rob (defraud, swindle), please (charm, delight).
Here again, the last three are not readily conjoinable with the others because of differences in aspect D. If we consider verbs with an 'opposite' meaning to please, etc., such as *upset, dismay, frighten,* we can see that these are much more readily conjoinable.

Subgroup P2u: $+ S_{part} + Ad_{inst}$: kill, murder, hit (slap, smack, strike, bash), please (charm, delight).

Subgroup P2v: $+ S_{part} + Ad_{neut}$: please (charm, delight).
If we try to conjoin Agentive and Neutral Adjuncts with these verbs, we obtain sentences such as *Mary was pleased by Tom and the scenery* which is somehow strange. The same is true for conjoining Instrumental and Neutral Adjuncts as in *Mary was pleased by/with Tom's tricks and the scenery.* It could not be claimed that either of these examples is 'impossible'. In fact, it

is unusual conjoinings of this type which are used by effective speakers and writers.

Subgroup P2w: $+S_{part} + O_{neut}$: show, give.

8.10. Group P3: Predicate fillers in Passive Voice; three overt GMs

Subgroup P3a: $+S_{aff} + Ad_{ag} + Ad_{inst}$: open (close, shut, lock), break (smash, shatter), hit (slap, smack, strike, bash).

These all seem to be conjoinable. The permutation: $+S_{aff} + Ad_{inst} + Ad_{ag}$ seems to be possible with all of these, although it may be more likely with some verbs like *hit* than others like *break*.

Subgroup P3b: $+S_{aff} + Ad_{ben-i} + Ad_{ag}$: give, donate.

Subgroup P3c: $+S_{aff} + Ad_{fact} + Ad_{ag}$: change (turn).

Subgroup P3d: $+S_{aff} + Ad_{inst} + Ad_{inst}$: change (turn).

Subgroup P3e: $+S_{aff} + Ad_{part} + Ad_{ag}$: give, steal.

Subgroup P3f: $+S_{ben-i} + O_{fact} + Ad_{ag}$: give.

Subgroup P3g: $+S_{ben-i} + O_{fact} + Ad_{ag}$: cook (bake).

Subgroup P3h: $+S_{ben-i} + O_{neut} + Ad_{ag}$: give, buy.

Subgroup P3j: $+S_{ben-i} + O_{neut} + Ad_{part}$: buy.

Subgroup P3k: $+S_{fact} + Ad_{ben-i} + Ad_{ag}$: cook (bake).

Subgroup P3l: $+S_{inst} + Ad_{loc-i} + Ad_{ag}$: smear (splash, daub, plaster, paint).

Subgroup P3m: $+S_{loc-i} + Ad_{inst} + Ad_{ag}$: smear (splash, daub, plaster, paint).

Subgroup P3n: $+S_{neut} + Ad_{ag} + Ad_{inst}$: look at (examine, view, peruse).

Subgroup P3o: $+S_{neut} + Ad_{ben-i} + Ad_{ag}$: give, donate, buy (purchase).

Subgroup P3p: $+S_{neut} + Ad_{part} + Ad_{ag}$: show, sell, let, give + to, rent, buy + from.

In general, a permutation $- + S_{part} + Ad_{ag} + Ad_{part}$ is possible.

Subgroup P3q: $+ S_{part} + Ad_{aff} + Ad_{ag}$: rob (defraud, swindle).

Subgroup P3r: $+ S_{part} + O_{aff} + Ad_{ag}$: give, send.

Subgroup P3s: $+ S_{part} + Ad_{ag} + Ad_{inst}$: kill, murder, please, hit (slap, smack, strike, bash).
In general, a permutation $- + S_{part} + Ad_{inst} + Ad_{ag}$ is possible.

Subgroup P3t: $+ S_{part} + O_{neut} + Ad_{ag}$: show, sell, give.

8.11. Group P4: Predicate fillers in Passive Voice; four overt GMs
Subgroup P4a: $+ S_{aff} + Ad_{fact} + Ad_{inst} + Ad_{ag}$: change (turn).

Subgroup P4b: $+ S_{ben-i} + O_{neut} + Ad_{ag} + Ad_{part}$: buy.
Permutation $- + S_{ben-i} + O_{neut} + Ad_{part} + Ad_{ag}$ is also possible.

Subgroup P4c: $+ S_{neut} + Ad_{ben-i} + Ad_{ag} + Ad_{part}$: buy.
Permutation to $+ S_{neut} + Ad_{ben-i} + Ad_{part} + Ad_{ag}$ is also possible.

8.12. Conjoinability of Predicate fillers
As can be seen from the three matrices and the remarks under 8.1–8.11, conjoinability by *and* of Predicate tagmemes with certain fillers depends on a number of factors:

8.12.1. *B-aspects*
As already mentioned earlier, one of the prerequisites is that co-occurring tagmemes do not only match in their A-aspect (GF) but also in their B-aspect (GM).

8.12.2. *Implied Grammatical Meanings*
The importance of GM implications must not be overlooked, as they have a considerable influence on conjoinability. Appendix A gives a matrix showing those GMs which are always implied and those which are optional.

8.12.3. *C-aspects*
Although I have been stressing the meaning layer of the tagmeme, C-aspects (Lexical Forms) must not be overlooked. For instance, Adjunct tagmemes whose fillers start with different prepositions are not easily conjoined and make

conjoinability of Predicate tagmemes more difficult. Often, a rather clumsy effect is achieved.

8.12.4. *D-aspects of Predicate tagmemes*
D-aspects play their part in two ways. There is firstly the D-aspect of the filler itself. Fillers whose D-aspects are either very similar or strongly opposed often resist conjoining, except in special cases, e.g., in the case of *buy* and *sell* (and others) where a type of consecutiveness is introduced.

8.12.5. *D-aspects of co-occurring tagmemes*
. In addition, there is also the D-aspect of other tagmemes in the construction, particularly Subject and Object tagmemes. If they vary greatly, then Predicate fillers which match in every other way, still resist conjoining.

8.13. Examination of conjoinability on the basis of GF only
Another type of conjoinability, that of GF with same GF, for example Subject with Subject may also be examined. I shall confine myself to occurrences of one overt GM first with predicate fillers in the active voice and then in the passive voice, where I have claimed that certain predicate fillers may have different GMs occurring as Subject.

8.13.1. *Predicate fillers in Active Voice*

$+ S_{aff}$: the meat $+ S_{ag}$: the chef $+ P$: cooked,

*The meat and the chef cooked.

$+ S_{aff}$: the meat $+ S_{fact}$: the meal $+ P$: cooked,

*The meat and the meal cooked.

$+ S_{ag}$: Joe $+ S_{inst}$: the bullet $+ P$: killed,

*Joe and the bullet killed.

. However, it is true that *Joe and his knife killed,* seems more acceptable. Thus, if the Agent co-occurs with an Instrument indicated as being possessed by the Agent, an acceptable sentence is possible.

$+ S_{ag}$: Mary $+ S_{fact}$: the meal $+ P$: cooked,

*Mary and the meal cooked.

$+S_{ag}$: Joe $+S_{neut}$: the weather $+P$: are nasty,

*Joe and the weather are nasty.

This seems, at least, to be strange. Furthermore, *be nasty* with an Agentive Subject would occur in the Progressive Form, *is being nasty.*

8.13.2. *Predicate fillers in Passive Voice*

$+S_{aff}$: the peas $+S_{fact}$: the meal $+P$: were cooked,

*The peas and the meal were cooked.

$+S_{aff}$: the tree $+S_{part}$: Joe $+P$: were hit,

**The tree and Joe were hit.*

Even if we permute the two Subjects, *Joe and the tree were hit* sound strange, whereas: *Joe and Fred were hit* with two Participative Subjects or *The tree and the bush were hit* with two Affective Subjects seem to be acceptable.

8.14. Examination of conjoinability of Predicate fillers with different GM implications

Thus it would seem that different GMs appearing in the one type of GF do not freely conjoin. Also, Predicate fillers implying different GMs do not freely conjoin although they may co-occur with the same GFs. Thus

$+S_{GM-a}$: x $+P$: verb-b $+O_{GM-c}$: y

$+S_{GM-d}$: x $+P$: verb-e $+O_{GM-f}$: y ,

are not conjoinable to form

$+S$: $+P$: verb-b + verb-e $+O$: y.

For instance

$+S_{ag}$: Tom $+P$: hit $+O_{aff}$: Fred

$+S_{part}$: Tom $+P$: liked $+O_{neut}$: Fred,

are not conjoinable to give

*Tom hit and liked Fred.

It would seem that the less correspondence there is between GM implications, the less the likelihood of conjoining. If there is only one GM difference,
conjoining may be possible as in:

$+ S_{ag}$: Tom $+$P: built $+ O_{fact}$: the house

$+ S_{ag}$: Tom $+$P: destroyed $+ O_{aff}$: the house,

where the Objects have different GMs but where

Tom built and destroyed the house,

is a possible sentence. Or again, with Subjects having different GMs:

$+ S_{part}$: Tom $+$P: saw $+ O_{neut}$: the house

$+ S_{ag}$: Tom $+$P: bought $+ O_{neut}$: the house,

which gives: *Tom saw and bought the house.*

9. GRAMMATICAL MEANING BELOW THE CLAUSE LEVEL

9.0. Possible filler sets of Clause Level tagmemes

Fillers of Clause Level tagmemes may be phrases or clauses, including Relative Clauses and Reduced Clauses. I use the term Reduced Clauses here as this is the term used by Becker but I do not imply therby that there has necessarily been any reduction from any more full type of clause. In fact, the term Dependent Clause might be more appropriate. In general, my illustrations have simply a noun or a determiner plus noun as the fillers of Subject, Object and Complement functions, and Prepositional Phrases consisting of a preposition plus a noun or determiner plus noun as the fillers of Adjunct functions, except in the case of Ad_{loc} where a Locative Adverbial could be used.

In this chapter, it is my purpose to show that the previously mentioned Clause Level tagmemes may be filled by phrases having within themselves GM relationships. For example, we would consider Becker's (1967:111) example: *The building of the boat (by John)* as consisting of: $D_{sp} \; H_{pr} \; Sb_{fact} \; (Sb_{ag})$ where H_{pr} stands for Predicatival Head to indicate its relationship to Predicate at Clause Level. The internal structure of such phrases which are related to clauses will depend on the Predicatival Head just as the internal structure of the clause depends on the filler of the Predicate tagmeme.

9.1. Phrase or Reduced Clause

Becker (1967: 111) seems to distinguish between Reduced Clauses such as *John's building of the boat* and *For John to build the boat* and phrases such as *The building of the boat (by John)* and *John's building of the boat*. However, he does not make clear his reasons for distinguishing these pairs and particularly for distinguishing between the first and the fourth.

All four include forms of the verb, either infinitive or -ing form. However, there is the difference that the first two may be expanded by the addition of adverbials whereas the second two may be expanded by the addition of adjec-

133

tival forms. Thus we may have:

> John's *energetically* building the boat (surprised everyone),
> For John to build the boat *energetically* (would surprise everyone),
> The *energetic* building of the boat (by John) (surprised everyone),
> John's *energetic* building of the boat (surprised everyone).

It is of interest to examine each of the above types of reduced clause and phrase in relation to GM:

For S to V... type Reduced Clause.

It would seem that any Non-reduced or Independent Active Clause may have a related Reduced Clause of this type. Thus:

Jack resembles his brother.	For Jack to resemble his brother (would surprise me).
There is a red roof on that house.	For there to be a red roof on that house (would mean that they must have just painted it).
Jim is happy.	For Jim to be happy (would amaze me).

S's v-ing... type Reduced Clause

It will be necessary to consider the acceptability of various GMs as Subject. This type of reduced clause is related to the Active Independent Clause type and so it will also be necessary to consider the Reduced Clause related to Independent Passive Clauses separately.

$+S_{aff}$ The door's opening (surprised us).

This type of Reduced Clause is acceptable to some but seems slightly unnatural.

$+S_{ag} + O_{neut} + Ad_{part}$ Harry's (suddenly) renting the house from Victor (made us suspicious).

It would seem that an Independent Active Clause with S_{ag} has a related Reduced Clause.

$+S_{ben-i} + C_{neut}$ Tom's having a car (made us think he must have won a lottery prize),

$+S_{fact}$ The meal's cooking (so quickly) (surprised everyone).

This seems 'strange' and is of very dubious acceptability.

$+S_{inst} +O_{part}$ — This pistol's killing Sykes (would seem to have been unlikely).

This is of very doubtful acceptability. However: *The bullet's hitting the window (was unfortunate),* where we have $+S_{inst} +O_{aff}$ would seem to be more acceptable.

$+S_{neut}$ — The meat's smelling (so foully) disappointed Mary,

$+S_{neut} +C_{neut}$ — Jack's (surprisingly) resembling his brother (causes confusion).

The first seems more acceptable than the second which seems most unlikely. In general, the type of verb which may co-occur with S_{neut} in an Active Clause has a related noun which is more likely to occur than the -ing form. Thus, a phrase: *Jack's (surprising) resemblance to his brother* in the second case or: *The meat's foul smell* in the first would be far more likely.

$+S_{part} +Ad_{inst}$ — Joe's dying of a gunshot wound (shocked us all).

In general, Independent Clauses with $+S_{part}$ would seem to have a related Reduced Clause of this type.

It would seem that any Active Clause with S_{ag}, S_{ben-i} or S_{part} has a related Reduced Clause of the Subject's v-ing type. Clauses with other Subjects would seem to be far less likely to have such a related Reduced Clause.

S's being v-en type Reduced Clause

It would seem that any non-reduced or independent Passive Clause may have a related Reduced Clause of this type if the Subject is human. Some non-human but animate Subjects are possible with some speakers, especially if the Subject refers to a domestic animal. Thus:

Fido's being hurt by a car upset Mary.

In general with inanimate Subjects, the Reduced Clause of this type would seem unacceptable. Thus:

The book's being sold to Sam (was unfortunate),

seems 'strange'.

S.'s v-ing ... type Phrase

It would seem that any Non-reduced or Independent Active Clause with Agentive Subject may have a related phrase of this type. Thus:

> Black & Co's selling of the book (took a long time),
> Blogg's (constant) stealing (landed him in gaol).

Any Subject but Agentive seems very dubious or completely unacceptable as may be seen by the following examples:

$+S_{part} + O_{neut}$ *Mary's (unexpected) smelling of the meat (sickened her).

Thus, it would seem that a transformation to a S's v-ing type phrase would be an extra discovery criterion for Agentive Subjects.

The v-ing of X ... type Phrase

This type of phrase is related to Passive Clauses according to the following formula:

Independent Passive Clause	*Phrase*
$+S: x + P: v ...$	The v-ing of x ...

We may examine this type of phrase according to the GM of the Subject in the related Passive Clause.

Independent Passive Clause	*Phrase*
$+S_{aff}$	The locking of the door (takes place at 10 p.m.).
$+S_{fact} + Ad_{ben-i}$	The cooking of a meal for the visitors (took a long time).
$+S_{loc-i} + Ad_{inst} + Ad_{ag}$	The smearing of the wall with paint by Fred (was very careless).
$+S_{neut} + Ad_{ag}$	The showing of the film by Fred (will take place later).
	The learning of this lesson by Fred (will help him pass the exam). (This seems rather awkward, but it is difficult to say whether it is unacceptable.)
	The looking at/examining/viewing/perusing of the document (took place at noon). Of these, only *viewing* seems acceptable.

Independent Passive Clause	*Phrase*
$+ S_{neut} + Ad_{ag}$	The giving/donating of the books by the chairman (will take place this evening). Here, *donating* is unacceptable.

It would seem that if we have a Passive Clause with Neutral Subject, a related phrase of the: The v-ing of x... type is possible unless there is a related noun which would be substituted for the v-ing form. Thus, instead of: *examining, perusing, donating,* we would have: *examination, perusal, donation.* In fact, this is probably true with other Subjects, but it would seem that verbs which may co-occur in the Passive Voice with Neutral Subjects often have a related noun as with: *examine, peruse, donate.*

$+ S_{inst} + Ad_{loc\text{-}i} + Ad_{ag}$	The smearing of paint on the wall by Fred (was most unfortunate).
$+ S_{part} + Ad_{ag}$	The robbing of the rich by Robin Hood (displeased the Sheriff of Nottingham).
$+ S_{part} + Ad_{aff} + Ad_{ag}$	The robbing of the rich of their money by Robin Hood ... (This certainly seems less acceptable, no doubt because of the repetition of *of*.)
$+ S_{ben\text{-}i} + O_{neut} + Ad_{ag}$	The buying for Mary of a watch by Fred (seems rather extravagant). This is a very awkward construction.

In general, it would seem that any Passive Clause with Affective, inner-Locative, Instrumental, Neutral or Participative Subject has a related phrase of this type unless there is a noun which would be substituted for the v-ing form of the verb.

A more extensive and intensive examination of Reduced Clauses and Participial and Infinitive Phrases and their relationships to independent clauses would probably show up further restrictions dependent on GM.

9.2. Grammatical Meaning relationships in Pure Phrases

I shall now briefly consider GM relationships in phrases which do not contain any infinitive or -ing form of the verb. Becker (1967: 126 ff.) has considered pure phrase constituents in the order: Determiners, Subjuncts [1] and

---

[1] A Subjunct tagmeme is a tagmeme at phrase level which is subordinate to the Head tagmeme and qualifies it.

Heads. However, it may be convenient to consider these in reverse order. In fact, it may be necessary to consider the Head and Subjunct together because it is the relationship of these which determines the GM of the Head and of the Subjunct.

9.2.1. *Grammatical Meanings of Pure Phrase Heads*

As mentioned above, it is the combination of the Subjunct and Head which gives rise to the various GMs. Thus, a phrase such as: *A worker for charity* might be considered as containing: $H_{ag} Sb_{ben}$. Again, *A farm worker* might be considered as having: $Sb_{loc} H_{ag}$. On the other hand, in: *A fat worker,* the head, *worker* cannot be considered as H_{ag} as he is *not* a worker for, in or with fat.

It is only at Word Level, that *worker* might be considered as *necessarily* containing an Agentive constituent, i.e. the affix: *-er*. At Phrase Level, it is no more *necessarily* an Agentive Head than a place name is a filler of a Locative function at Clause Level. *London*, in *London is a city* is not a S_{loc} as we do not have a related *It is a city in London.* Similarly at Clause Level, *The hammer lay on the table* does *not* include *hammer* as S_{inst}. The fact that we *do* say *London is a city* and not (normally) *London is an elephant* or *London became an heiress* is a matter of Aspect D or Lexical Meaning.

Some examples of different kinds of Head are given below according to the subdivision: Affective, Agentive, Benefactive, Factitive, Instrumental, Locative, Neutral, Participative.

H_{aff}	The broken *window.* The recently sent *letter.*
H_{ag}	The charity *worker.* The lino *layer.*
H_{ben}	The home *owner.* The *possessor* of a fortune.
H_{fact}	A cooked *meal.* A well-built *house.*
H_{inst}	A well-used *tool* (possibly *used* is the only filler which would co-occur with H_{inst}).
H_{loc}	A guest *house* (This is dubious as it could be considered as $H_{purposive}$, *a house for guests.* However, it could be considered as: *a house where guests stay.*)
H_{neut}	A fat *boy.* An unseen *intruder.* A widely shown *picture.*
H_{part}	The disappointed *suitor.* A dismayed *student.*

It will have been noticed that the Subjuncts to H_{aff}, H_{fact}, H_{inst} and two of the Subjuncts for H_{neut} are 'past participial forms of the verb'. These we can consider as Predicatival Subjuncts (cf. Predicatival Heads in section 9.0). It would seem that H_{aff}, H_{fact}, H_{inst} must occur with Subjuncts of this type or, in some cases of the -ing type.

Another point which will have been noticed is that in some examples a modifier had to be added to the Predicatival Subjunct (Sb_{pr}). Thus, we cannot have: *The sent letter, *The built house, *A shown picture or, for that matter, *A seen intruder. Becker (1967:140) has a short but interesting discussion of this and refers to Fillmore's use of the terms: affiziertes Objekt and effiziertes Objekt. Fillmore has, of course, related these two terms to his Objective and Factitive cases respectively. Becker suggests that where the head is the *affectum* we can have both: *A skilfully stolen car...* and *A stolen car...*, whereas if the Head is *effectum,* we can have: *A skilfully built car...* but not *A built car...*

This is true, but the matter is certainly more complicated. It is true that if we have a Factitive Head (H_{fact}) we do need a descriptive as well, except where the same Head could occur as H_{aff} as in the case of *cook, bake.* Thus, we do not have: *The built house or *The manufactured car or *The constructed shed. It is, of course, very much a matter of Aspect D. Why would anyone *want* to say: *A built house, The manufactured car* or *The constructed shed*? Houses *are* built, cars *are* manufactured and so on. However, this does not invalidate the argument. There might seem to be counter examples. What about: *manufactured articles, a cooked breakfast*? Here, it happens that not all articles *are* manufactured, not all breakfasts *are* cooked.

However, when we turn to the 'affiziertes Objekt' type, the problem is considerably more complicated. Why can we have: *A stolen car* (Becker's example), *The broken vase, The murdered man, The injured woman, The (be)loved parents* but not *The killed man, *The kicked woman, *The lifted box* (but we may possibly have *The lifted paint*), *The thrown ball or *The touched vase?*

These latter all seem to be of the 'affiziertes Objekt' type and so there must be some other constraint which operates here. Lyons (1968:350 ff.) in his discussion of the term 'ergative' and of causatives classes certain verbs as 'ergative' verbs. His examples are: *move, change, grow, develop, open, close, start, stop, begin, break, crack, split, tear.* With all these verbs, we can have occurrences of the type: *John moved the stone* or *The stone moved.* With *some* of them, we may also have occurrences such as: *John moved* (Lyons 1968:359).

With *grow, develop, open, close, break, crack, split, tear,* we can have the patterns:

John grew the flowers.	The flowers grew.	The grown flowers.
John developed the film.	The film developed.	The developed film.
John opened the door.	The door opened.	The opened door.
John closed the door.	The door closed.	The closed door.

John broke the vase.	The vase broke.	The broken vase.
John cracked the glass.	The glass cracked.	The cracked glass.
John split the seam.	The seam split.	The split seam.
John tore the trousers.	The trousers tore.	The torn trousers.

Thus it would seem that when we have clauses of the type: $+S_{ag} +P +O$ and the filler of the Predicate may also occur in clauses of the type: $+S_{aff} +P$, both clauses being in the Active Voice, then we may also have phrases of the type: Det Sb: Past Participial Form of Verb H_{aff}. We must now examine *change, move, start, stop, begin* to see why these do not fit into the preceding pattern.

| John changed the tyre | *The tyre changed. | *The changed tyre. |

Here, quite obviously, as we do not have *The tyre changed*, we do not have *The changed tyre. Of course we have clauses of the type *Mary has changed* but this is not related to *John has changed Mary*. In fact the only type of trio is possibly

| John changed his opinion. | John's opinion changed. | John's changed opinion. |

However, it is dubious whether we can consider *John* as Agentive here, but rather as Participative. Phrases related to Transitive Active Clauses with S_{part} will be discussed later. We may now consider *move*.

| John moved the stone. | The stone moved. | *The moved stone. |

The difference between this and our previous set of eight verbs seems to be that although the Subjects of them are S_{aff} in the second column, the Subject of *move* with no Object does not necessarily have to be S_{aff}. We certainly may have a S_{ag} in this position, e.g., *John moved*. This is also the case with: *start, stop, begin*. Thus it may be that for phrases of the type: Det Sb: v-en H, the verb, if it takes an Affective Object in Transitive Clause, must also occur with S_{aff} in Intransitive Clauses. Furthermore, the Subject of the corresponding Intransitive Clause must not optionally be Agentive instead of Affective.

We can now see why *The lifted box, *The thrown ball and *The touched vase do not occur. This is because we do not have *The ball threw, *The vase touched or *The box lifted. However, we do have *The paint lifted* and so: *The lifted paint* seems more acceptable.

We are still left with the problem of Becker's example: *A stolen car.* Certainly we do not have clauses of the type *A car stole* related to *Joe stole the car.* Therefore, why may we have *A stolen car?* Notice that we do *not* have *A taken book.* A possible answer to this is that although *take* does not imply taking from someone, for example, we can have *Mary took a saucepan from the shelf,* steal does imply this. We would consider that the person from whom something is stolen fills a Participative function. Similarly, we may have *The purloined book, The borrowed book* as *purloin* and *borrow* both imply the GM Participative.

We may now consider why we can have *The murdered man, The (be)loved parents* and *The injured woman* but not **The killed man* or **The kicked woman.* The case of *The (be)loved parents* is different from the others. Here, although *love* implies the GM Participative, this refers to the person who loved. Parallel to this would seem to be *The feared dictator, The hated enemy, The despised informer.* In the other cases, there is a Participative Head.

In general, it would seem that we can have phrases of the type D_{sp} Sb: v-en H_{part}. Other examples besides *The murdered man* and *The injured woman* are *The frightened child, The disappointed suitor, The dismayed student.* Why then do we not have **The killed man* or **The kicked woman*? Taking the second example first, as we also have clasues of the type *Joe kicked the chair* where *the chair* would be O_{aff} but do not have **The chair kicked* it would seem that we do not have a phrase **The kicked chair* and therefore not **The kicked woman.*

The matter of *kill* is more problematical. Lyons (1968:352–353) seems to suggest *kill* and *die* as 'alternative, syntactically-conditioned, phonological realizations of the 'same' verb'. The problem here is that although *kill* has the meaning (usually) of 'cause to die', *die* is not *kill* minus causative. At least, *die* could seem to co-occur with 'causes' of death as in: *He died of tuberculosis, She died of a broken heart.* For the present, the fact that we do not normally have **The killed man* must simply be considered as an irregularity with the explanation that one would hardly *want* to say *The killed man* because we have *The murdered man* to cover 'the man intentionally and unlawfully killed', *The dead man* covers dying from other causes. Within this, if we want to know further, we want to know whether he dies of 'natural causes' or how specifically he was killed. Furthermore, when there is a contrast, a phrase including *killed* is acceptable as in:

The killed man lay in the gutter but the injured
man crawled to the roadside.

9.2.2. Grammatical Meanings of Subjuncts

Subjuncts have, unavoidably, been introduced in section 9.2.1 but we may briefly review these according to their GMs. In addition to the range of Subjuncts, Affective through to Participative, we may have Predicatival Subjuncts as illustrated in section 9.2.1 in the case of *broken, dismayed,* etc. The following list is illustrative of various types of Subject:

Subjunct in Pre-Head position		Head (with GM)	Subjunct in Post-Head position
Aff:	building	repairs (Pred)	
		repairs (Pred)	to the building
Ag:	John's	production (Pred)	
		(e.g., of a book)	
		(this) work (Pred)	of John's
Ben:	John's	book, car, etc. (Neut)	
		(the) book (Neut)	of John's
			for John
Fact:	(John's) book	production (Pred)	
		(the) production (Pred)	of a book
Inst:	pick and shovel	work (Pred)	
		work (Pred)	with a pick and shovel
Loc:	Melbourne('s)	buildings (Neut)	
		buildings (Neut)	in/of Melbourne
		flowers (Neut)	of/on the wattle
Neut:	red	book (Neut)	
		book (Neut)	of a red colour
Part:	John's	foot, head (Neut)	
		love (Pred)	
		(the) love (Pred)	of John (for...)
Pred:	broken	chair (Aff)	

Generally, the co-occurrence possibilities of the various Subjects and Heads according to GM are similar to the co-occurrences at Clause Level. In addition, there are what might be called 'Manner Subjunct' which are related to Manner at Clause Level. For instance: *The badly broken chair* has a Manner Subjunct, *badly,* a Predicatival Subjunct, *broken* and an Affective Head, *chair.* On the other hand, with a Predicatival Head, we could have a Manner Subjunct as in: *The vicious killing.* Becker (1967:137) discusses the matter of: *The man sleeping peacefully on the couch* and seems to dislike the analysis of *peacefully* as a Manner Subjunct because 'peacefully' and 'on the couch' are, as he says:

'clearly adjuncts of the predicate 'sleeping' and its deleted subject rather than subjuncts of the head 'man'.' He is quite right in that *peacefully* and *on the couch* refer to *sleeping* but if we analyze this as:

$$D_{spec} \; H_{part} \; Sb_{pred} \; Sb_{man} \; Sb_{loc} ,$$

then the fact that we have a Sb_{pred} will indicate that the two other Subjuncts refer to this. We may have a convention that any other Subjunct will be related to a Predicatival Subjunct in the same way that at Clause Level a Subject, Object, Complement or Adjunct is related to the Predicate. If we have: *the man on the couch*, this will be analyzed simply as:

$$D_{spec} \; H_{neut} \; Sb_{loc} .$$

It would therefore seem unnecessary to derive *The sleeping man* from *The man who is sleeping.* The two are related as would be shown by our formulae but we do not need to posit that the one is derived from the other.

A discussion of Determiners is beyond the scope of this work but there are obvious relationships between the occurrences of Determiners and various GMs. Thus with a clause of the type:

$$+ P: \text{there be} \; + S \; + Ad_{loc\text{-}i} ,$$

we may have only the 'Indefinite Article' co-occurring with the Head of the Subject and not the 'Definite Article'. Thus we may have *There is a red roof on the house* but not **There is the red roof on the house.*

10. CONCLUSION

10.0. Language universals and language particulars

It has become obvious from the preceding chapters that all the four aspects (i.e. A, B, C and D) of a tagmemic model must be considered if a grammar is to generate acceptable sentences in any one language.

It is felt that aspects B and D are language universal and that aspects A and C are language particular. Leaving further discussions of D and C aside and concentrating on the GF/GM dichotomy, it is considered very likely that most if not all languages have the same set of GMs (aspect B) but not the same set of GFs (aspect A) and that furthermore the co-occurrence of the GMs with GFs differs considerably from language to language.

Another matter that must be considered as language particular is the co-occurrence of certain GMs with others in clause constructions or even the regular manifestations of a GM with a particular GF or the fact that in certain languages GMs never appear together with certain GFs under specific circumstances.

For instance, in various Australian aboriginal languages, an Instrument may not appear as Subject. One cannot translate *The boomerang hit the man* into an active clause in one of these languages. One may have *The man hit the man with a boomerang,* for example in Pitjantjatjara *watiŋku wati kaḻiŋka ruŋkaṇu* but not *kaḻiŋka wati ruŋkaṇu.* However, one can have a sentence like *maḻu punkalpaji kuḻataŋka wakan-yaŋka,* literally *Kangaroo(s) fall (habitually) spear-with speared – Kangaroos fall when they are speared,* where no Agent is mentioned.

In German, for instance, the GMs Participative/Benefactive are most certainly present in the GM implications of Predicate fillers such as *geben* (give) *schenken* (donate) etc., but there is a different GM–GF relationship in this language, i.e. the GMs Participative and Benefactive do not combine with the GF Subject, e.g.,

Die Mutter gibt *dem kleinen Nachbarjungen* einen roten Ballon,
Ein roter Ballon wurde *dem kleinen Nachbarjungen* geschenkt,

but not

Der kleine Nachbarjunge wurde einen roten Ballon gegeben.

(The only possible construction would be with the 'Nachbarjunge' in the
Dative Case, i.e. GF Indirect Object, e.g.,

Dem kleinen Nachbarjungen wurde ein roter Ballon gegeben/
geschenkt).

10.1. Outline of a Clause Level generative grammar

Any clause generating device must take into account GF and GM.

A model of the following type is suggested:

(1) *Select GMs.* I do not wish to assert that four is the maximum number of
GMs permissible in any GM implication of a Predicate filler. This number just
happened to be the maximum in our exemplification.

(2) *Match GMs to Predicate fillers.* Thus, if we had selected GM Neutral and
GM Participative, *see* would be a possibility as its GM implications are +neut
+part (see 7.1.3).

(3) *Select overt GMs and match these to GFs.* For instance, we might select
only +neut to appear overtly. This would be a possibility with *see* but it would
not be so with some other Predicate fillers. With *see,* if + neut is the only GM
appearing in a GF, then the filler of the Predicate tagmeme must be in the
passive and the GM Neutral must co-occur with the GF Subject.

To exemplify this further, we may consider the first four Predicate filler
examples in ch. 7:

7.1.1.   open

7.1.2.   cook

7.1.3.   see

7.1.4.   show.

With these, the following GM combinations are possible according to the formulae at the beginning of each section:

GM implications: + aff + ag
                  + aff + inst
                  + aff + ag   + inst
                  + ag   + fact
                  + ag   + fact + ben-i
                  + neut + part
                  + neut + part + ag.

We can arrange these in a matrix which is read from left to right:

Implied GMs

One GM	Two GMs	Three GMs
+ aff 1, 2	+ ag 1, 2 + inst 1	+ inst 1
+ ag	+ fact 2	+ ben-i 2
+ neut	+ part 3, 4	+ ag 4

where the numbers refer to the numbering of the Predicate fillers in ch. 7.

Thus, if we selected + aff, we may have *open* or *cook* but if we choose + aff + ag + inst, we may choose only *open.*

We then need to find out what GMs may be overtly omitted. This may be done by a matrix of overt GM occurrences:

Overt GMs

One GM	Two GMs	Three GMs
+ aff 1, 2	+ ag 1, 2 + inst 1	+ inst 1
+ ag 2	+ fact 2	+ ben-i 2
+ fact 2		
+ neut 3, 4	+ part 3, 4	+ ag 4

Thus we find that although in the matrix of implied GMs, Predicate filler 2, *cook* was shown as implying + aff + ag, or + ag + fact, in the matrix of overt GMs, it is shown as possibly occurring with + ag only.

Each Predicate filler could be listed in a lexicon with its implied GMs and its overt GM possibilities. There would also be a need to show how these GMs may occur with certain GFs.

Thus, following our groupings in Active and Passive Clauses in ch. 8, *open* would appear with the following entries (referring to the sets of which it is a member):

$$1a, \quad 2a, \quad 2f, \quad 2k, \quad 3b,$$
$$P1a, \quad P2a, \quad P2d, \qquad P3a.$$

From these, it could be seen that *open* may co-occur in a clause construction with the following tagmemes:

(1) *In Active Clauses*

with	$+S_{ag} +O_{aff} (+Ad_{inst})$	according to 2a or 3b
	$+S_{aff} (+Ad_{inst})$	according to 1a or 2k
	$+S_{inst} +O_{aff}$	according to 2f

(2) *In Passive Clauses*

with	$+S_{aff} (\pm Ad_{ag} \pm Ad_{inst})$	according to P1a, P2a
		P2d or P3a

10.2. Some further problems

10.2.1. *The portmanteau tagmeme*

Here we have a case where two GFs and two GMs are contained in one tagmeme with one filler only. This doubling-up of aspects A and B occurs when one clause is embedded within another. For example in a sentence like

Joe helped Tom cut the timber,

Joe would have the GM Agentive and the GF Subject, *timber* would have the GM Affective and the GF Object, *Tom* would have the GM Participative and the GF Object in relation to *help* but the GM Agentive and the GF Subject in relation to *cut*.

The following formula will illustrate this:

$$+S_{ag}: Joe \; +P_{X1}: helped + \begin{bmatrix} +O_{part} \\ +S_{ag} \end{bmatrix} : Tom \; +P_{X2}: cut \; +O_{aff}: the\ timber.$$

Portmanteau
tagmeme

It might be argued also that *Joe* is an Agent in relation to *cut*. The most common interpretation of the sentence would be that Joe helped Tom cut the timber by himself cutting some. However, this is not necessarily so. He may have done other work which helped Tom's cutting without actually himself cutting the timber. We must, however, show that Tom has the GMs Participative and Agentive and the GFs Object and Subject. Thus it would seem that whenever a clause is embedded in this way, the GMs and GFs combine in one portmanteau tagmeme.

10.2.2. *One GF with two or more GMs*

This issue has not been discussed up to now but it seems that one GF may have two (and perhaps more) GMs in various ways:

(a) I have stated that a verb like *listen to* implies the Agentive GM in relation to the person listening. However, the Agent is obviously also Participative. Here, it might be considered that a clause like

Fred listened to the birds,

should be considered as

$$+S_{ag+part} \quad +P \quad +O_{neut} \; .$$

(b) One Predicate filler which is mentioned by Fillmore (1968b:377) is *blame*. It might well be worth considering this now. Fillmore illustrates *blame* in two examples:

Harry blamed his failures on Mary,
Harry blamed Mary for his failures.

Are we to consider *Harry* as Agentive because one can say

Blame Mary for your failures,

or as Participative because blaming is not the sort of action (not necessarily overt) like *looking at, examining, listening to* which one actually initiates?

Again, is Mary to be considered as Participative because often if a person is blamed, that person knows that he or she is being blamed? This is not, however, implied by *blame*. One can blame someone who will never hear of the blaming and one may not desire that he ever hear of it. For example:

Joe blamed the boss for his failure,

where Joe has a strong desire that the boss never hear of his remarks. Furthermore, one can have, for example:

> Harry blamed the weather for his failures,
> Harry blamed his failures on the weather.

Thus, we might say tentatively that *Harry* fills a Participative Subject and Mary a Neutral Object. The problem still remains of what GM to assign to *his failures.* Any discovery procedure such as: *For what purpose did Harry blame Mary*? seems strange. The most suitable discovery question would seem to be: *For what reason did Harry blame Mary*? Thus, we might consider a GM Reason. The same discovery question would also obtain answers like:

> Harry blamed Mary because she was lazy.

This differs in that Harry blamed Mary for something which may not affect him whereas in our previous example, Harry blamed Mary for being responsible for his (Harry's) failures. Furthermore, we do not have:

> *Harry blamed Mary for her laziness.

Again, our suggested discovery question would hardly work with:

> Harry blamed his failures on Mary.

This would hardly be a response to:

> Why (for what reason) did Harry blame Mary?

Tentatively, we could consider that *blame* does imply the GM Reason and that if the head of the Neutral tagmeme is not referred to (by a Possessive: his, her, etc.) in the Reason tagmeme, then we may have

$$+S_{part} \quad +P \quad +O_{neut} \quad +Ad_{reason}$$

Harry blamed Mary for his failures,

or

$$+S_{part} \quad +P \quad +O_{reason} \quad +Ad_{neut}$$

Harry blamed his failures on Mary,

$$+ S_{neut} \qquad + P \qquad\qquad + Ad_{part} \qquad + Ad_{reason}$$

Mary   was blamed   by Harry   for his failures.

Another solution would be to consider Mary as having a Neutral GM in relation to *blame* and an Agentive GM in relation to an abstract Causative. This would probably give a greater insight into the implications of *blame*.

10.3. The GF–GM dichotomy and its significance

A type of semantic Deep Structure has been suggested in the previous pages that can be incorporated into the four-aspect concept of the tagmemic unit as suggested by Pike and developed by Becker. I have changed Becker's interpretation by establishing criteria of definition of the various GMs (B-aspect) which made them to some extent more independent of the C and D-aspects of unit and put them into a relation to the Predicate (and with it to the Predicate filler).

It is suggested that in this way certain universal concepts may be obtained which would be invaluable in inter-language investigation. All too often advocates of an 'anti-universal' approach have used 'surface structure' criteria for the basis of their argumentation. In seeing and accepting the GM–GF dichotomy, it can now be argued that there *are* universal concepts within each language as well as those concepts (GF) which are to a large extent language particular. Both have their values and neither one should be disregarded at the expense of the other.

APPENDIX A

Matrix showing GM implications of Predicate fillers
GM implications and Predicate fillers discussed in this work (with the exception of *have* and *be*).

Symbols used:

+   obligatory GM.

++   two of the same GMs are obligatory.

±   optional GM.

v   either one or the other of the other of the indicated GMs is obligatory, but *not* both.

± *v*   either one or the other of the indicated GMs may occur optionally, but *not* both.

±, +* optional GM, but only when it is present can be GM marked (*) appear.

± (*) optional GM, but its occurrence is dependent on the presence of the GM marked +*

v, +* an obligatory GM is in an exclusive relationship with another GM (also marked *v*) *but*, in addition, a GM marked (*) is dependent on it. See explanations above.

v (a) an obligatory GM is in an exclusive relationship with another one marked also *v*(a).

v (b) an obligatory GM is in an exclusive relationship with another one marked also *v* (b).

In the case of *bake* and *cook*, (1) and (2) refer to the two GM-implication formulae for these Predicate fillers.

153

Matrix showing GM implications of Predicate fillers

	Affective	Agentive	Benefactive (inner)	Factitive	Instrumental	Locative (inner)	Neutral	Participative
admire							+	+
assassinate		+			+			+
bake	+(1)	±(1) +(2)	±(2)	+(2)				
bash	ν	+			+			ν
borrow		+					+	+
break	+	±			±			
buy		+	±				+	+
change	+	±,+*		+	±(*)			
charm		ν,+*			±(*)		ν	+
close	+	±			±			
cook	+(1)	±(1) +(2)	±(2)	+(2)				
daub		+			+	+		
defraud	+	+						+
delight		ν,+*					ν	+
detest							+	+
discover							+	+
dislike							+	+
donate	ν	+	+				ν	
enjoy							+	+
examine		+			±		+	
execute		+			+			+
exterminate		+			+			+
find							+	+
give	ν(a)	+	ν(b)				ν(a)	ν(b)
hit	ν	+			+			ν
injure		+			+			+

Matrix showing GM implications of Predicate fillers (*continued*)

	Affective	Agentive	Benefactive (inner)	Factitive	Instrumental	Locative (inner)	Neutral	Participative
kill		+			+			+
know							+	+
learn		v					+	v
lend		+					+	+
let		+					+	+
like							+	+
lock	+	±			±			
look at		+			±		+	
look like							++	
murder		+			+			+
notice							+	+
open	+	±			±			
paint		+			+	+		
peruse		+			±		+	
plaster		+			+	+		
please		$v,+$*			±(*)		v	+
purchase		+	±				+	+
rent		+					+	+
resemble							++	
rob	+	+						+
see							+	+
sell		+					+	+
send	+	+				v		v
shatter	+	±			±			
shoot		+			+			+
show		±					+	+
shut	+	±			±			

Matrix showing GM implications of Predicate fillers (*continued*)

	Affective	Agentive	Benefactive (inner)	Factitive	Instru-mental	Locative (inner)	Neutral	Partici-pative
slap	v	+			+			v
smack	v	+			+			v
smash	+	±			±			
smear		+			+	+		
smell		±v					+	±v
splash		+			+	+		
steal	+	+						+
strike	v	+			+			v
swindle	+	+						+
view		+			±		+	

BIBLIOGRAPHY

Works cited

Becker, A.L., 1967. *A generative description of the English subject tagmeme.* Ph.D. Dissertation, University of Michigan.

Boost, K., 1955. *Neue Untersuchungen zum Wesen und zur Struktur des deutschen Satzen.* Berlin.

Brend, R., 1968. *A tagmemic analysis of Mexican Spanish clauses.* The Hague: Mouton & Co.

Drach, E., 1939. *Grundgedanken der deutschen Satzlehre.* 2nd ed. Frankfurt/Main.

Erben, J., 1968. *Deutsche Grammatik,* Frankfurt/Main: Fischer Bücherei.

Fillmore, C.J., 1968a. 'The case for case'. In: Bach and Harms (eds.): *Universals in linguistic theory.* New York: Holt, Rinehart and Winston Inc.

Fillmore, C.J., 1968b. 'Lexical entries for verbs'. *Foundations of Language,* vol. 4, no. 4, 373–393.

Longacre, R.E., 1964. *Grammar discovery procedures: a field manual.* (Janua Linguarum, No. 35). The Hague: Mouton & Co.

Lyons, J., 1968. *Introduction to theoretical linguistics.* London: Cambridge University Press.

Tesnière, L., 1966. *Eléments de syntaxe structurale.* Paris: C. Klincksieck.

Other works

Anderson, J., 1970. 'The case for cause: a preliminary enquiry. *Journal of Linguistics,* vol. 6, no. 1, 99–104.

Bach, E., 1968. 'Nouns and noun phrases'. In: Bach, E. and Harms, R.T. (eds.): *Universals in linguistic theory.* New York: Holt, Rinehart and Winston, Inc.

Becker, A.L., 1967. 'Conjoining in a tagmemic grammar of English'. In: Dinneen, F.P. (ed.), *Monograph series on languages and linguistics,* No. 20. Washington: Georgetown University Press.

Chomsky, N., 1957. *Syntactic structures* (Janua Linguarum, no. 4). The Hague: Mouton & Co.

Chomsky, N., 1964. 'A transformational approach to syntax'. In Fodor J.A. and Katz, J.J. (eds.): *The structure of language.* Englewood Cliffs: Prentice-Hall, Inc.

Chomsky, N., 1964. 'Degrees of grammaticalness'. In: Fodor, J.A. and Katz, J.J. (eds.): *The structure of language.* Englewood Cliffs: Prentice-Hall Inc.

Chomsky, N., 1965. *Aspects of the theory of syntax.* Cambridge, Mass.: The M.I.T. Press.

Fillmore, C.J., 1966.'A proposal concerning English prepositions'. In: Dinneen, F.P. (ed.): *Monograph Series on Languages and Linguistics* no. 19. Washington: Georgetown University Press.

Katz, J. and Postal, P., 1964. *An integrated theory of linguistic description.*Cambridge: The M.I.T. Press.

Lakoff, G., 1965. *The nature of syntactic irregularity.* Cambridge: Harvard Computational Laboratory.

Langacker, R.W., 1968. *Language and its structure: some fundamental linguistic concepts.* New York: Harcourt, Brace & World.

Langendoen, D.T., 1969. *The study of syntax: the generative–transformational approach to the structure of American English.* New York: Holt, Rinehart and Winston, Inc.

Longacre, R.E., 1960. 'String constituent analysis'. *Language* 36, 1.

Longacre, R.E., 1965. Some fundamental insights of tagmemics. *Language* 41.

Longacre, R.E., 1967. 'The notion of sentence'. In: Dinneen, F.P. (ed.): *Monograph Series on Languages and Linguistics* 20. Washington: Georgetown University Press.

Lyons, J., 1967. 'A note on possessive, existential and locative sentences'. *Foundations of Language* 3, 390–396.

Pike, K.L., 1962. 'Dimensions of grammatical constructions'. *Language* 38.

Pike, K.L., 1964. 'Discourse structure and tagmeme matrices'. *Oceanic Linguistics* 3.

Pike, K.L., 1966. *Tagmemic and matrix linguistics applied to selected African languages* (Final Report for U.S. Office of Education, Contract No. OE-5-14-065). Ann Arbor: Center for Research on Language and Language Behavior.

Pike, K.L., 1967. *Language in relation to a unified theory of the structure of human behavior.* 2nd ed. (Janua Linguarum, no. 24). The Hague: Mouton & Co.

Platt, J.T., forthcoming. *The Gugada dialect.* Canberra: Australian Institute of Aboriginal Studies.

Postal, P., 1964. *Constituent structures: a study of contemporary models of syntactic description.* IJAL Publication 30 of the Indiana University Research Center in Anthropology, Folklore and Linguistics 30, 1 (pt. III).

Robinson, J.J., 1970. 'Case, category and configuration. *Journal of Linguistics,* vol. 6, no. 2, 57–80.

Stockwell, R.P., Schachter, P. and Hall Partee, B., 1968. *Integration of transformational theories of English syntax.* Los Angeles: University of California.

Svartvik, J., 1966. *On voice in the English verb.* (Janua Linguarum Series Practica, 63). The Hague: Mouton & Co.

GRAMMATICAL MEANINGS

(Main references are indicated on the pages below)

GRAMMATICAL FORMS

(Main references are indicated on the pages below)

INDEX

161